The Love Song of Bugs Fluffernut

My Year with a Wild Rabbit

A Memoir by

ANGELA HAVEL

Cover mixed-media drawing and frontispiece pencil drawing by Cyra Cancel

cyra12cancel@yahoo.com

http://bycyra.ebsqart.com

www.zazzle.com/by_cyra

ISBN: 1499308612

ISBN 13: 9781499308617

Library of Congress Control Number: 2014908083

CreateSpace Independent Publishing Platform

North Charleston, South Carolina

William Stafford, excerpt from "Traveling through the Dark" from *Ask Me: 100 Essential Poems*. Copyright © 1998, 2014 by the Estate of William Stafford. Reprinted with the permission of The Permissions Company, Inc. on behalf of Graywolf Press, Minneapolis, Minnesota, www.graywolfpress.org.

DEDICATION

To those who love and protect animals

ACKNOWLEDGEMENTS

Thanks to Kelley Hunt for his encouragement in seeing this project through. Thanks also to my mother, Mary Havel, my father, Edward Havel, brother Edward Havel, Jr., and sister Debbie Huff.

Thanks to Heather Jones, Sigrid Macdonald, Ashia Wehbe, and John D. Williams for editorial comments, to Heather Jones for copy editing, and to Cyra Cancel for her art.

Thanks to fellow writers Ashley Bonine, Terri Brown-Davidson, Giselle Hager, Season Harper, Nancy McCabe, Laura Patterson, and Randy Rhamy for their support.

I acknowledge for their inspiration Richard Adams, author of *Watership Down*, R. M. Lockley, author of *The Private Life of the Rabbit,* and William Cowper's poems about hares and rabbits.

Finally, I acknowledge with gratitude my animal friends, past and present, who make life worth living.

Table of Contents

$\mathcal{E}$ PIGRAPH

Well—one at least is safe. One shelter'd hare
Has never heard the sanguinary yell
Of cruel man, exulting in her woes.
Innocent partner of my peaceful home,
Whom ten long years' experience of my care
Has made at last familiar; she has lost
Much of her vigilant instinctive dread,
Not needful here, beneath a roof like mine.
Yes—thou mayest eat thy bread, and lick the hand
That feeds thee; thou mayest frolic on the floor
At evening, and at night retire secure
To thy straw couch, and slumber unalarm'd;
For I have gain'd thy confidence, have pledged
All that is human in me to protect
Thine unsuspecting gratitude and love.
If I survive thee, I will dig thy grave;
And, when I place thee in it, sighing say,
"I knew at least one hare that had a friend."

-- William Cowper ~ from "The Garden"
Book III of the poem *The Task (1785)*

MARCH 2012

BIRTH

If you've ever saved an animal's life, you know the secret song of the universe.

I learned this on a humble farmyard in north central Kansas. Picture yourself at the cusp of spring, when nature is bursting with promise. Spring 2012 had sprung precociously early in the prime wheat-growing area of the United States. By mid-March, our yard vibrated with color. Lilacs that normally bloomed in early May stood misted with lavender clusters, drawing bumble-bees into their sweetly intoxicating fumes. A redbud tree by the vegetable garden splashed magenta against the blue sky. Grape hyacinths and pink parrot tulips glowed like fire against the lawn.

A clan of barn swallows, who returned to our farm every year since I could remember, appeared two weeks ahead of schedule, burbling their twitter-warble while rebuilding mud-and-sticks nests in corners of the porch.

And the ultimate harbinger of spring—the birth of cotton-tail rabbits—began.

I had just finished digging a lettuce bed when heart-rending staccato squeals echoed near the house. I knew that sound—a baby cottontail rabbit. I ran to find the bunny hanging limply from the powerful jaws of my yellow Labrador, Sophie.

"Sophie!" I yelled. She dropped her head and deposited the creature to the ground, a fall of several inches. It was about the size of a mouse, and the same dun color. Stunned but alive, the rabbit wriggled to right itself. Its eyes were sealed shut. Only the stubby tail, blunt head, longish ears, and those distinctive squeals signaled its genus.

At such moments, the world exits my brain, and a rush of pure panic washes over. Years before, I had rescued from the jaws of a cat a newborn cottontail, immediately returning the kit to a clearly visible nest—a small depression in the grass near the foundation of the corn crib. This time the kit was too far from its point of origin. I had no clue where the nest was.

I have got to think, I told myself. *I have got to know what to do.*

Sophie and my miniature poodle Opie circled the kit, sniffing it menacingly. I carefully picked it up, pulled the front of my T-shirt forward to make a cradle, and hastily donned a leather glove. On the off chance I found its home, I figured the mother would better accept the kit without human scent.

With the kit perfectly still and quiet in my gloved palm, I wandered the yard, looking for the nest. My dogs and cats could find such elusive spots with their acute senses, but I was denied such knowledge.

Normally I would have seen rescuing a vulnerable creature as a favorable opportunity, given my love of animals. But at this particular time, I was in the midst of preparation for an auction, ten days away, of my father's farm miscellanea. His death a year earlier vortexed my mom and me into a whirlpool of responsibility. Upon his death, I immediately sold my home in southwest Nebraska where I taught college English courses online and lived quietly with my dogs and cats, and moved, at the age of 47, to the farm where I grew up. If ever a widow needed help, Mom did. The crop-producing land had been sold years earlier—we were down to fifty acres. The problem was, at some point in the 1990s my father's collection of farm machinery large and small, iron equipment, tools, vehicles that didn't run, and assorted detritus no one else would bid on at the many farm auctions he'd attended over the years had amassed into a plague. He could not part with a scrap. Anyone who's seen "that kind" of yard knows what I mean. The ten acres on which our house stood, plus forty acres of pasture across from our yard, and a second home a half-hour away in Fairbury, Nebraska, allowed lots of room to spread the accumulation, and our mess wasn't as unsightly as other farm yards I've seen in these parts, but to the untrained eye, the piles looked like—there's no other way to say it—*junk*. Half the mass was modestly valuable, but the shortest distance to that value was not a straight line. My direct requests to Dad, years before his death, that we start clearing out the saleable items invariably met with resistance.

A year before he died, I asked Dad a final time, "So what do you want me to do with it?"

He knew what "it" meant.

"You call up an auctioneer, and they come in and take care of it, no problem." His offhand manner belied his discomfort at being confronted with the question.

Dad's "no problem" prediction was a bust. After his funeral, I saw the handling of his collection as MY problem. When my brother in California said, after I told him I needed his help, "What's the hurry in cleaning it up? It's been sitting there for years!" my heart sunk. Mom and I were going to have to manage alone. Mom, at 79, was not in shape for hard labor, and so the job fell onto me.

A couple of months after we buried Dad, I started with the most cut-and-dried task: sorting and cataloguing Dad's eighty-five guns, two-thousand boxes of cartridges, and several trailer loads of gun parts, with four months of cataloguing help from our neighbor Roland, and several days of appraisal help from Norm, one of dad's gun buddies. I don't like guns and found this job distasteful, but the payoff was creating a cushion for Mom.

After the gun auction, I steeled myself for the clean up of the farm yard. The saleable items ranged from the behemoth—a two-ton truck, an Allis-Chalmers tractor that didn't run, and a herd-of-elephants-sized iron scrap pile that sold "as is"—to breadbox-or-smaller-size "too numerous to mention" items, as the auction ads read, with all sizes in between: plows, cultivators, mowers, cars, pickups, iron stoves, forges, push cultivators, welding equipment, hay rakes, Grim Reaper-style scythes, you name it. Big items were often buried by small items, or vice versa; everything had to be dug out of Dad's nooks and crannies, dusted off, and put in some kind of order. The "too numerous to mention" items ended up on five flatbed trailers for bidders to gather around.

Dad believed in hard work, and that belief was so strong it reached beyond the grave. At my core I was a farm kid, but I'd spent most of my adult years living for myself, away from our farm, with little responsibility besides my teaching career and a midlife first-home purchase. I was physically soft, and my inside wasn't in the best shape either: I felt hollow and embittered, missing some crucial element of humanity. Scratch a cynic and you find an idealist deep down; apparently, I couldn't be scratched deeply enough. I cited a particularly dour strain of Eastern European DNA for my glass-half-empty view of life, and likened the clean up job ahead of me not as a challenge to be met with gusto, but as the rolling-a-boulder-up-a-hill labor of Sisyphus. Or maybe Hercules' cleaning of the Augean stables was more accurate. But I was on no hero's journey. Acres of piled iron and a quarter-of-a-football-field-size machine shed packed to the rafters awaited me. While surveying the shed's contents, I lighted on a once-proud bright green John Deere baler, now encrusted with thirty-five years of dust, imprisoned two-thirds of the way into the shed by surrounding junk. That baler became the brass ring I reached for. Its neighbors were a '73 Cadillac with a sprung hood, an old farm pickup that didn't run, a camper from the '60s, and a bull-sized grain thresher. Nestled within were snarls of broken wooden chairs, a pandemonium of iron tools, and a mobocracy of oddments. Oh, and a dead opossum to boot, rotting and stinking, lying in one of the narrow maze-like aisles when I led the auctioneers on their first visit to see what Dad had wrought. The creature had likely died because he couldn't find his way out.

"Have you ever seen anything like this?" I asked one of the auctioneers.

"Not for years, and not quite like this," he replied, in a quiet tone that appeared to result from shock. I quickly saw that the two auction preppers he brought with him weren't going to cut it. One said he had a bad back, and the other looked like he wanted to get the hell out of the yard. I called the auctioneer the next day to tell him I'd find my own help.

Call *American Pickers*, everyone told me. Ha. I've watched the two guys on that show look for treasure in the sheds, barns, and yards of rural America, but never have I seen them pick through a shed like Dad's. One look at the entrance blocked with rubble and they would have fled, flummoxed.

Who was I going to find? There weren't many strong, reliable day-labor types in our area to help me. A neighbor recommended an auction house out of Lincoln, Nebraska, who was known to capably handle, for a hefty fee, the dirty work, but I didn't trust putting Dad's collection, even if a lot of it was junk, in the hands of outsiders. The Midwestern farmer's mantra I grew up with, that you grit your teeth and take care of your business, bubbled inside.

I soon found the premonitions I'd had before Dad's death, about not having the grit to handle his estate, manifested as anger after his death.

The clean up forced me to scale back on my online English teaching—a career I took pride in. I had no social life. I'd never been much of a social type anyway; growing up in a rural area had solidified my tendency towards solitude.

The problem wasn't just the junk. The problem was, I felt adrift in that sea of junk, profoundly alone, and leagues from the shore.

The rabbit I held in my palm—so new to the world it wasn't afraid of me—took all thoughts of junk sorting mercifully away. Nestling as delicate as a bird's egg, and not much bigger, the kit's tightly-sealed-shut eyes created a wall of mystery. I kept checking for the barely perceptible rising and falling of its pinkish-brown abdomen. Its breathing seemed the life force of the universe in miniature. A pureness emanated from its form, fresh from the hand of a Creator. It couldn't have been more than a couple of days old.

As I continued looking for a nest equivalent to a needle in a haystack, traversing a triangle from house to barn to granary, then along a row of Eastern Red Cedars behind our house, the heady scent of wild plum blossoms perfumed the air, punctuated by a waft of wild onions. How could the unsurpassed wonder of this new life coexist with nature's dark side, the constant threat of death? The dark side could win this battle, and claim the orphan.

"Hang in there, buddy," I whispered to the kit.

As if to confirm that the kit's life hung precariously in the balance, I saw with a jolt an imprint of Sophie's incisor at its neck. Suddenly, the William Stafford poem "Traveling through the Dark" came to mind: the speaker finds a pregnant deer struck dead by a vehicle, feels a live fawn still warm inside her, yet pushes the doe over an embankment to get her out of the way of other cars. Stafford's speaker says he "thought hard for us all" in sacrificing the unborn fawn.

I thought hard for myself. Responsibilities around the approaching auction loomed. Saving the kit's life would require time and patience. I hated myself for the thought, but I considered finding an out-of-the-way spot to leave the kit to its fate. Just as quickly as it came, that idea curdled like rotten milk; I would not be able to live with myself if I didn't try. Fate had entrusted to me a sleek furry slip of a life. A force beyond my reckoning told me not to sacrifice this new life to what I selfishly deemed important human cares.

I headed back to the house and showed the kit to my mother, who was peeling carrots at the kitchen table.

"Oh no," she said.

"Oh yes," I replied.

"How can you? The auction...."

"How *can't* I?"

Mom knew better than to argue.

My first instinct was to make a nest for him—for some reason I already thought of the rabbit as a male; later I discovered upon closer examination I guessed right. I placed him gently in a cigar box on the bathroom counter off Dad's old bedroom, now my room, making sure to shut the bathroom door against any visits by my cats and dogs. I found a medium-size cardboard box and headed back outside to gather fresh prairie grass growing behind our house, circling it into a nest to line the bottom of the box. Then I grabbed a small wad of polyester-fiber stuffing from my sewing supplies, and placed that in the middle of the prairie grass. A mother rabbit lines her nest with her stomach fur, but the polyester would have to do. Underneath the nest, I set a thick towel and a heating pad on low, placed under half the box so he could crawl off the heated spot in case he got too warm.

A comma-shaped cipher of some meaning I didn't yet know lay silent and still on his artificial nest, waiting for me to make the choices that would save him. There was no time to waste. He needed food.

I found a small nursing bottle in my pet medicine box. The Internet became invaluable for instant information; I learned that rabbit's milk is one of the richest in nature, that baby rabbits feed once or twice daily, and that the closest I would come to rabbit's milk was kitten milk replacer. I raced fifteen miles to the local vet's office to buy some, measured out a couple of tablespoons, mixed this with water, then added several drops of rich cream and acidophilus, the same bacteria in yogurt, which helped replace the digestive enzymes a mother rabbit's milk contains. The site I'd consulted recommended acidophilus *granules* because they dissolved easier. They were supposedly readily available at any health food store, but being nowhere near health food stores, powdered acidophilus in capsules from the local pharmacy would have to do. I used a spoon and toothpick to mash and mix part of a capsule into each feeding.

I gave up on the pet nursing bottle when I discovered it was impossible to get the right size X cut into the nipple so milk would flow without flooding the kit's mouth. Plus, all the nipple tips, even the tapered one designed for a rabbit, were way too big for his pencil-tip-sized mouth. A small syringe with the needle removed worked. At first the little guy, eyes still shut tightly against the world, didn't want to accept the tip of the syringe. This is the point where most people lose orphaned baby rabbits—they simply refuse to eat. I sensed my rabbit was a fighter, though, with the same conviction I sensed that I could save him. I was determined to get some milk down him. With patience, we succeeded. I had to maintain careful control of my thumb while slowly pushing the plunger, to avoid a flood in his face that could drown him. A few times, more milk than he could swallow flowed out of his mouth, but for the most part the milk went down, and while I wasn't feeding him the recommended 10-15 milliliters per day—he drank 2 to 2.5 milliliters at each feeding, three times a day—I hoped it would be enough.

The powdered acidophilus created unexpected humor: after accepting a mouthful of formula, he'd flick his clover-stem-width tongue first to the left, then to the right, over and over, mushing around in his mouth the grainy texture of the powder. He had likely nursed on his mother's milk for at least a couple of days before I found him, and I knew my attempt to recreate that milk didn't equal nature's genius. I felt badly for him, but couldn't help laughing at the cuteness of that tiny tongue flicking. I hadn't laughed in a long time, and felt a bond starting between us.

Mom watched me mix the rabbit formula every morning in the kitchen before I headed out to sort items for the auction, but didn't ask how the rabbit was doing. She wasn't the compelled-by-unknown-forces-to-take-in-orphaned-baby-rabbits type. Also, she quickly grew frustrated about the location I'd picked for the rabbit's temporary home—the bathroom where she showered.

"He's doing quite well; I know you're curious," I told her a couple of days after his rescue.

"That's good. I'll need to use the shower later today. Is the bathroom out of commission?"

"He's in a box on the counter—no problem, you can use the shower. Just don't jostle the box by mistake!" My tone was more perturbed than necessary, but I couldn't help being frustrated with her. I wanted her to understand. Call me a crazy romantic, but now that I'd committed to the challenge, saving this baby rabbit's life meant nothing less than redemption for my tattered soul.

His sealed-shut eyes gave his face a strangely wizened look. Did the stress of his predicament cause that look? I tried to imagine the unknowable workings of an animal's mind, and came up short. I cooed softly to him while feeding, mistakenly thinking this would soothe him. I learned later, after more online reading, that this was a mistake—he would have preferred silence while feeding. Getting out of my human consciousness and into this wild animal's consciousness didn't come naturally. Even those of us who believe we're "animal people" are too anthropocentric. If I'd thought more carefully about the kit's realm, it would have occurred to me that only the sucking sounds of his siblings and the ambient sounds of nature would accompany his feedings. Still, I persisted throughout his first weeks talking to him while feeding him. "Good rabbit," I'd say, or "Here you go, little guy," as if that would help him live. His acceptance of my well-meaning but wrong-spirited attempts stood as testament to his adaptability; he could have spurned my care entirely and succumbed to fate. I suspect this is what happens to the 85% of orphaned cottontails who don't make it—they simply reject the artificial human environment they are subjected to. Who could blame them? At least our house was quiet, which I counted as a plus in the rabbit's chances.

Every morning during the first week of his life, before my day's work, I'd rise at 6:30 a.m., open the bathroom door silently, breathe in the sweetly delicate baby-fur smell, then peer into the cardboard box on the counter. There he lay sleeping, breathing rhythmically, those mysterious eyes still sealed shut like a kitten's at birth. Cottontails' eyes open at approximately ten days, and I waited with anticipation for the windows to his soul to reveal themselves.

Each day I found him breathing and alive created a well of joy deep inside I'd thought lost during childhood, that kind of forget-the-world joy I'd felt only a few times before, like the time my younger brother Ted, our neighbor Vicki, and I got into a rotten apricot fight and I festooned Ted's favorite Dallas Cowboys T-shirt with a glorious orange splotch. Weird memory to light on, I know, but nailing my brother's shirt after he yelled "You throw like a girl!" filled my chest with effervescence. That's exactly how it felt—my rabbit's perseverance was a catalyst, dissolving my world-weariness.

My orphan also gave me motivation to tackle the dirty auction prep work with vigor, and I finally found a guy to help me: Rick, owner of a small auction house in Hebron, Nebraska, who declared sorting through the junk was like "Christmas every day" to him. He was available on a limited schedule, but his help was invaluable. In the midst of sorting for the farm auction, he and I also started hauling contents from Mom and Dad's second residence, a Victorian-style reconverted funeral home mom had purchased fifteen years earlier for a steal to house Dad's "runover," to Rick's Quonset for weekly mini-auctions. The home's 6000 square feet featured fourteen rooms and a basement packed with more of Dad's hodge-podge of furniture, tools, and retro gadgets—stuff I didn't know the value of. In the midst of sorting, when I'd hold up a seemingly no-account item and ask "Is this worth anything?" Rick would look at the object and intone soberly, "It'll sell."

A week or so before the big farm collectibles auction, one of Dad's friends, a collector of Indian artifacts named Jim, helped me burn unsaleable rotten wood and other junk in three large piles. Jim told me about countless times as a kid he'd tried to save orphaned cottontails without success; his face lit up when I told him my orphan was still alive after a week in my care. I was gaining confidence daily that he would pull through, yet while talking to Jim, I found myself expressing some corrosive doubt.

"He's not out of the woods yet," I told him. "I'm waiting to name him, so I don't jinx him."

"Sounds like you're doing the best you can," he said thoughtfully. I asked if he'd like to see him, and we took a break to walk to the house. I could tell Jim was decent by his look of admiration at the rabbit's meek form. Most men in this area see wild rabbits as game or pests, unworthy of respect.

Miracles don't happen unless you're willing to see them. A heart no bigger than a jot, encased in a tiny envelope of fur, continued beating despite overwhelming odds. My hard-shell cynicism split open as I witnessed the beginning of a miracle. Mom saw it. Jim saw it. Our neighbors the Baxters saw it—both their kids, Bryan and Grace, smiled in delight at my rabbit. My exboyfriend Kelley, who I still chatted with occasionally, sensed it. Even the secretary at the vet's office where I purchased the kitten milk replacer blurted incredulously, "That rabbit is still alive?" when I asked, ten days after my first purchase, for a second can of formula.

The day his eyes opened, I gazed with wonder into his unfettered soul. Those dark-brown eyes shone clear and bright, and I caught the first whisper of an exquisitely thrumming melody, just out of reach but promising a revelation.

$\mathcal{A}$ P R I L

$\mathcal{H}$OW $\mathcal{B}$UGS GOT HIS NAME

The chimera of our early spring settled fully on the earth, digging its warmth into the soil. I planted bare-root Rugosa roses and dwarf peach, pear, plum, apple, and cherry trees on the 15th, and by the 30th they were profusely leafing. The honeyed air hung thick and lazy over the yard.

My rabbit got a little more formula than usual the morning of the auction—as much as he would take—and I thought about him all day while neighbors, collectors, and iron mongers bid on the vast assortment of nostalgia representing Dad's life. Once all the stuff had been sorted and set out for display, it didn't look so junky, and I was almost proud of the wide range of items for sale.

Most antique collectors—they don't like the word "junk"— are friendly folk. One told me he sometimes flew his Cessna to auction sites, finding landing strips in nearby pastures. He admitted his family called him a hoarder. His wife, a pleasant sort who taught English, added the tidbit that his hobby wasn't one she'd have chosen, but she'd learned over the years to appreciate the history of farm life by way of collectibles they'd purchased. Talking with this friendly, progressive couple and others who'd bonded over their love of historical artifacts gave me a new perspective on my father's hobby. Although I hadn't ever talked to him about the masses he'd piled—except to bug him about when we'd clean them up—I now realized his collection was treasure to many.

Corn shellers, century-old iron machinery, push cultivators created lively bidding. Old bathtubs went for $40, forges went for $50-70, a dingy red fire hydrant brought $70. Iron wheels of the type placed decoratively in yards brought $10-30 each. I'd washed the dirt off the John Deere baler to restore its distinctive green color, but it needed major repairs and brought only $400. Iron bed frames, anvils, old signs advertising seed corn brands, car horns, hubcaps—all found a new home. I even learned from a couple of guys who'd come to preview items the day before the auction that the thumb-size chunk of iron placed in a hole at the top of an anvil is called a "hardy" and that this small item is highly sought after by iron-forge collectors. The machine shed was still half-full of items to be auctioned at a later sale, and they wanted to nose around inside. I hesitated, knowing Dad would have told them "no" outright, but I didn't want to sound off-putting to future buyers, and told them they could look for a few minutes. Excited as kids in a candy store, they plowed their way through the narrow pathways between Dad's stacks, stopping every few seconds to comment on some item that caught their eye, headed to a corner of the shed where they saw some anvils, obviously on a "hardy hunt." They didn't find any, but one of them declared helpfully, "If you find some hardies when you sort this stuff, watch out so people don't walk off with them; they're a small item that can be easily pocketed." I thanked them for the tip, and later googled "anvil hardy" to see exactly what one looked like.

I'd hidden away before the auction an old kitchen sink Dad had dragged into the yard from one of his many farm sale excursions. I didn't want it appearing on the sale bill or at the auction. The trite pun "everything but the kitchen sink" came to mind, and I wanted to avoid hearing the snickering comment, likely from an older man in overalls, "Hell, they even got a kitchen sink!" Even that sink would have sold, though.

The auction started strong, on an unusually warm day for early spring—a hot wind blew. My excitement at seeing the nearly one-hundred trucks and trailers dotting the small pasture by our driveway, hearing the auctioneer's amplified chant, and smelling hot dogs cooking in the concessions van parked on our lawn kept me animated while I watched our yard empty. Sophie wandered the crowd, tail wagging, approaching everyone who held food for a handout, ignoring my admonishments. Opie was inside the house for the day; his miniature poodle-size made him too vulnerable with all the vehicles moving around the yard. After I let him out for a mid-morning pee, I held him while walking through the crowd for a few minutes to let him see the action, but he became nervous and was happy to go back inside.

The morning flew by, but the heat and the sheer volume of inventory tired out even the stalwart; by mid-afternoon the crowd had dwindled. The final item up for bid—an antique well pump—sold at 4 p.m. with a straggling group of ten or so bidders left.

I wasn't able to get away for my rabbit's evening feeding until 5:30 p.m., several hours later than usual. Although Mom would have gamely tried to feed him had I asked, I chose not to. I thought of him as mine, loyal to my feeding style.

He was one hungry bunny that evening.

"Done with the big auction, little guy," I told him, smiling down at his smooth furry face and irresistible dark-brown eyes as I positioned the syringe into his mouth. We had got his feedings down to a science and didn't lose a drop. He slurped down an extra syringe of milk, and I stroked his belly softly with one finger, as I'd learned early on from the online sites that said this action replaced the mother rabbit's licking to stimulate digestion.

"I think you're going to make it, little guy. We gotta think of a name for you."

❧ ❧ ❧

There was no time to rest after the first auction. Another smaller auction at the farm loomed, set for the third week in April, and again the sorting commenced.

"You're going to put your back out lifting that iron. People never recover from serious back injuries!" Mom called after me as I left the house one morning. "Why don't you let Rick handle it himself?"

My first instinct was to retort "Worry about your own back!" but my mood had improved, and I managed to hold my reply to "I'm in this for the duration, mom!" I banged the door closed harder than I should have, but I wanted to emphasize those words. Truth was, my body was becoming harder and stronger with daily physical labor. I felt better than ever.

⋖: ⋖: ⋖:

Before I could think of a name, Kelley, the ex-boyfriend, a farm boy and long-haul trucker who had once rescued an orphaned fawn, and who had taken a devoted interest in my rabbit, dubbed him "Bugs" with such an air of assurance I couldn't nix the name for lack of originality. Bugs he was. My ten-year relationship with Kelley had been stormy, and I'd never thought I could remain friends with an ex, but Bugs was a magic elixir: our communication was friendlier when we discussed his progress. I wanted a part in naming him too, and added a last name, Fluffernut, in honor of his quickly-growing fur, but mostly he went by Bugs.

Early in the month, as a way to unwind from the day's labor, I started recording videos of Bugs to post to YouTube. Kelley wanted to *see* Bugs' progress. The first video shows me feeding Bugs when he was around two weeks old. I asked Mom to film us. It was too dark in Bugs' master-bathroom home, so I brought him to the dining room, a brightly-lit space, for the first time. Despite the new environment, plus my droning to Mom about how to hold the camera, and, as I noticed later, my pulling the syringe out of his mouth several times to reposition it, tiny Bugs handled himself with aplomb. A patient and dear personality was emerging. He had utterly and completely wormed his way into my heart. The thought of releasing him was becoming anathema, despite the orphaned cottontail care websites indicating that trying to domesticate a wild rabbit beyond the age of weaning is "cruel."

That first video led to more: Bugs eating greens for the first time, then Bugs eating fresh pea pods, an apple slice, and a mini carrot. Each time I uploaded a video of Bugs, I was delighted to see him represented with all the other bunnies on YouTube. There's a thriving group of rabbit lovers on the Internet, I found. You can find Bugs' YouTube clips by searching "Bugs the wild bunny."

At about three weeks, Bugs graduated from a smallish box on the bathroom countertop to a bigger box on the bathroom floor. I still marveled at his minuteness, but each day he was gaining in size. He was now about four inches long, with ears the size of pussy-willow catkins. His coat, a solid taupe-ish brown, started developing a camouflaging ticking of grey, white, buff, and black. His baby's-fingernail-size blunt nose wriggled irresistibly, and his pea-size eyes sparkled.

I started offering him tender greens from the yard—dandelions, wild lettuce, clover—in addition to his daily milk. He'd settle himself into a perfectly still stance, then select a wild lettuce leaf and patiently chew it until it disappeared, then another, until the small pile was gone. I sensed he wasn't entirely comfortable with my watching him eat, but the lure of the greens won out, and he tolerated me sitting by his box, and even tolerated me filming him.

Even his poop was cute. Rabbit feces are pelleted, and because rabbits are herbivores, those pellets don't smell bad. Bugs' droppings were the size of miniature grains of rice; I'd find twenty or so daily, scattered on the towel in the bottom of his box, and removed them by shaking the towel outside. He didn't pee much yet, and I never smelled urea. Because his box was large, even with a few pee spots in the towel he had plenty of clean space to rest. When more than a few pee spots showed up, I'd replace the towel.

You may wonder, as I did, what may have become of Bugs' litter-mates. The average cottontail litter consists of four or five kits. No other baby rabbits were caught by my dogs or cats that spring, at least that I witnessed, and I predicted at least one of Bugs' brothers or sisters would have made it through the treacherous seas of our yard's other predators: coyotes, raccoons, barn owls, and hawks. Weasels and snakes kill rabbits too, although weasels aren't found in this area, and the snakes I saw in our yard were generally smaller garter snakes, which don't kill rabbits. Just to check, though, I googled "which snakes kill rabbits?" and found upsetting information, including YouTube subject lines revealing snake-lovers who uploaded videos of pythons and boas eating live rabbits. I got out of there quickly, siding with the comment that read, in answer to the question, "Do snakes eat rabbits?": "Yes, they can and it's horrible. DO NOT LET IT HAPPEN."

Let's say one of Bugs' sisters survived. She would have started venturing from the "form" or nest—a slight depression on the ground lined with the mother's stomach fur—at only two weeks old to nibble tender clover and grasses. At five weeks, she would be weaned and fully self-sufficient, beginning her short life. Because they are prey animals, the average wild cottontail survives, on average, only one and a half years, foraging for sustenance. Once weaned, cottontails select their area for grazing, usually no more than a small part of a grassy acre with cover nearby, and live out their days.

When I'd see a rabbit of Bugs' size near our yard, I'd immediately think he or she might be a litter-mate looking for a lost brother, before realizing that notion was the lingering effect of reading, at the impressionable age of fourteen, Richard Adams' *Watership Down,* the classic novel about a group of wild cottontails in south-central England, living on a down, or small pasture, who save themselves by their wits and teamwork. Such anthropomorphism is sentimental, I know, but I cannot help the tendency towards it. Despite Adams' fantastical take on rabbits, his basic premise that cottontails must stay warily alert at all times is true. I understood this wary alertness even more since Dad's death—I was now responsible for the safety of my mom, plus seven animals, including Bugs, against human and animal predators. In a rural, out-of-the-way place, both threatened. I now kept a gun in a bottom drawer of my clothes dresser, saved from Dad's collection—a .357 Highway Patrolman. My cousin Glen showed me how to load and shoot it, and encouraged me to target practice, but I never did. The cold hard steel of guns and their loud report rattled me. Dad had given up hunting in his later years, and used a gun only to shoot into the night sky to quiet coyotes howling, or to shoot a stray opossum or badger that wandered into the yard and threatened his dog or cats. I couldn't bring myself to shoot anything, even the sky. I told myself I would react quickly and competently if threatened with real danger, but underneath I questioned myself.

Sometime during Bugs' fourth week, when we held our second farm-collectibles auction, I could tell he was growing impatient with his formula. What a difference a month made. The morning of our second auction, I fed him two syringes of formula, then left him a good-sized pile of greens, and didn't worry too much that I wasn't able to check on him during the day.

At the beginning of Bugs' fifth week in the bathroom, I found him outside his box, in a corner of the room. My best guess is that he'd jumped onto the large towel I had draped over the box as a makeshift roof, then hopped across the towel and jumped to the floor. I hadn't yet seen him hop, though; he always stood stock still when I entered the bathroom.

To accommodate him, I cut a small entry hole in his box at one corner. He immediately started using that hole to leave his box and explore the surroundings of the bathroom. I would open the bathroom extra quietly each time I entered, hoping to catch him in mid-hop, and finally one day I did. His hopping was cuter than all get-out, and best of all, served as another major signal that Bugs was out of the woods and would make it to adulthood.

In addition to his daily milk and greens, I started offering him a couple of teaspoons of small alfalfa pellets, served in a pickle jar lid. Mixed within the pellets were tiny pink and green colored grains, like confetti, which the ingredients list labeled as "groats." Soon after I first offered the pellet/groat mix, I was amused to discover that little Bugs picked out just the pink and green groats to eat, leaving the alfalfa pellets untouched. I also set by his food a small jar lid of water, with the water level only 1/8" high so he couldn't accidentally drown in it. I never saw him drinking from it, but he must have, as it needed filling every other day. Once he started drinking water consistently, the pee spots proliferated, and I replaced the towel in his box with newspaper.

Near the end of April, after his fifth week, I weaned Bugs from milk. The wild rabbit care websites emphasized that when releasing a young rabbit back to nature, it's a good idea to place a dish of food and water in a protected spot to let the rabbit transition for several days. I considered this option. The words "it is cruel to try to domesticate a wild rabbit" came back to me. I let the word "cruel" soak in, but I could not yet release Bugs. I knew letting him go free in our yard could result in death by one of my own domestic animals or the coyotes who yipped nightly and who sometimes encroached as close as fifty yards from the house. Finding a rural area free of predators, where he would live a long and happy life, was next to impossible. The truncated average lifespan of a cottontail in the wild distressed me beyond measure.

Our neighbor Ledona told me about a small zoo forty-five miles away with an area for wild rabbits that was supposedly safe; her daughter Diane had raised an orphan wild rabbit years before, and eventually released him there. I considered this option and even called the zoo to determine if a place to release rabbits still existed. It did, but I couldn't bring myself to take Bugs there. I was too attached; never seeing him again was a horrid thought.

Was I being cruel? I'd watch Bugs contentedly munching his growing panoply of fresh greens, a daily buffet of wild and tame lettuce, dandelion greens, radish tops, snap pea pods, clover, and brome grass, along with his groats and alfalfa pellets, and could not imagine a better life for him than I could provide. I also recognized my mindset as arrogant and out of keeping with nature's laws. The dilemma weighed on me.

Then Kelley told me about a friend of a friend in Nebraska who'd kept a rescued wild rabbit in captivity; that rabbit was now ten years old. If that person could do it, why couldn't I?

But in the dawn and evenings, when rabbits are active, I could sense Bugs' call towards the wild. He'd stand on his hind legs near the single small window in the bathroom and scratch at the wall, looking up as if to find some sign of the outdoors. He now darted from my hand to avoid my touch. This disappointed me in one way; still, I understood developing his wild instinct was in his best interest if I ever released him.

At any rate, he needed to be outside, and soon.

MAY

BUGS AND COCOA

I still don't understand what made me pursue finding a buddy for Bugs. I naively assumed, partly from reading Adams' novel *Watership Down*, that all rabbits are social. Only *European* rabbits are, turns out; they band together in warrens or burrows below ground, whereas American cottontails make their nests above ground, and when the mother weans her kits at five weeks, they generally roam on their own.

But in the blind way of humans trying to do what they feel is best for animals, I set about finding a buddy for Bugs.

I called our neighbor Shelley, who knew various animal lovers in the area, to ask about rabbits. She knew a guy who raised lots of rabbits for his kids' 4-H project, and who sometimes sold rabbits. When I called him to explain what I was looking for—a smallish male rabbit buddy for an orphaned wild rabbit—I was told, not surprisingly, he'd never heard of such a situation before. He said he may have the rabbit I was looking for among their Polish breed, which reached only three to four pounds at maturity. The Polish breed, known to be docile, sounded like a good fit.

I headed over to look at their rabbits, housed in their backyard in well-maintained hutches and buildings. So many! At least one hundred, maybe more, of various breeds and colors. They singled out a likely candidate named Cocoa, for his solid chocolate-brown coat. According to the breeder's daughter, who stated the fact so earnestly I had to smile, Cocoa was born with a "split penis," a deformity which made him unsuitable for showing or breeding, hence their desire to cull him from their herd. I immediately liked Cocoa and his split penis, and said I'd take him. I let the family know I would be a responsible rabbit caretaker by showing them the food I'd purchased, which included grains mixed with alfalfa pellets, and I told them about the hutch I had ready for him, and how I planned to put the hutch inside a bigger pen. They showed me their chicken enclosure, indicating how it could be adapted for rabbits, and I started formulating ideas for a pen in our yard.

The hutch I'd purchased was one of those put-it-together-yourself affairs, with nesting boxes suitable for chickens or rabbits. I'd ordered it online a couple of weeks earlier. Made in China, but of surprisingly good quality, it featured a hardwood-pine hutch with A-shaped roof, surrounded by a hail-screened "yard" about seven by four feet, with a door, and a short ramp leading from the yard to the hutch. Cocoa had been housed in a smaller hutch at his previous home, with occasional romps in a pen. This hutch would give him considerably more room. Rabbits are meant to hop!

Sure enough, Cocoa liked his new hutch, hopping many laps around the yard of the enclosure as soon as he touched the ground. His laps were, as you may have guessed, monitored by my four cats, who circled the perimeter of the enclosure like chum-attracted sharks. I trained Cocoa to go up the ramp to the hutch by holding a "buddy stick"—a lollipop for rabbits, with various grains stuck on with honey. At first Cocoa was hesitant, but with a few hunks of the buddy stick placed at intervals on the ramp, he soon hopped right up, and from then on, he hopped up and down the ramp as if it were a game.

For the time being, Bugs stayed in the bathroom. He was now eating just his alfalfa pellet-groat mix and a large pile of greens daily, and when I refilled his food and water, I'd sit and visit with him, telling him he was a good rabbit.

My plan was to give Cocoa a few days to acclimate to his new home, and more importantly, let him acclimate to my two dogs and four cats, then introduce Bugs to the pen.

If you ever decide to introduce a rabbit to an existing dog and cat family, be prepared for a show. The rabbit hutch stood in the middle of our yard where Mom and I could see it from the kitchen window, and quickly became a focal point for us as well as ultra-compelling "television" for my dogs and cats, who congregated along the perimeter for a glimpse of Cocoa. Upon seeing the hopping brown bunny, my cat Duane immediately jumped on the roof of the hutch, Othello clawed at the hail screen sides, Boots meow-raowed insistently, and Rocky, my shyest, best-behaved, and laziest cat, circled the hutch warily and tirelessly, in a burst of activity I hadn't seen from him in months.

Opie set up a constant yapping designed to shred my nerves, and Sophie followed suit, in a contralto woofing.

The animal circus had come to our farm.

I imagined the cats asking each other "What *is* it?" and the dogs answering "Doesn't matter! It's a weird hopper! We don't like it!" The lot of them, cats and dogs, were clearly motivated by an ages-old instinct to capture prey.

Cocoa, with typical bunny aplomb, tried his best to ignore the chaos, but he couldn't help but be rattled. The constant barking of the dogs and circling of the pen by the cats would drive even the most even-tempered creature insane. After a few minutes, I brought all six dogs and cats inside, against their and my mother's will; she would have been happy if they lived outside all the time.

I had to find a solution, and guess what—my father's junk came in handy. He'd collected all manner of old screen doors and wooden doors, storing them in the chicken coop, granary, and barn. We'd sold some of them, but not all. I sought out six of the best I could find, and fashioned them into a crude "view-blocker around the hutch" structure, wiring the doors to steel posts driven into the ground at the corners and halfway points on the long sides of the pen. After an hour of configuring and wiring, I arrived at a workable solution—a structure that blocked the dogs' and cats' view of Cocoa on all sides, except for a foot-wide section, because I didn't want to entirely block Cocoa's view to the lawn.

The morning I walked into the bathroom to find Bugs on the bathroom counter peeing on my makeup tray, various rice-sized poop pellets scattered across the sink and soap dish to boot, signaled a turning point. He had leaped three feet to get to that counter top. I could not delay any longer getting him outside. Cocoa had been in his new pen only four days at this point, but it would have to be enough of a breaking-in period.

Catching Bugs was not easy. I tried a cat carrier with a treat inside, but Bugs' natural wariness prevented his entering. I ended up covering him with a large Tupperware bowl and sliding a piece of heavy cardboard underneath. I apologized for upsetting him, and hurriedly moved him to the pen, my mother holding the front door open for me. She'd felt usurped by Bugs' presence in the house, and was more than ready for his departure.

Bugs entered the great outdoors with quiet grace. I imagined his little heart racing as I carefully opened the hutch yard door and watched him hop inside. The wind in the leaves of the hackberries, elms, and oaks overhead sounded like ocean waves, a mesmerizing lull. A chorus of birds twittered dulcet notes in the branches above the pen. Bugs' pinky-sized ears pricked up. After hopping a few feet, he stood erect on his hind legs, prairie-doglike, his head perfectly still.

Those ears! Fuzzy oblong antennae, capturing his world.

He was already tuning in to the song of the universe—our planet spinning on its axis—a music only wild creatures hear, greater than a symphony.

Cocoa was enclosed in the "house" part of the hutch; I was planning to introduce him to Bugs gradually. At first, Bugs hopped around the yard of his new home in what appeared to be something of a daze—the natural world buzzing all around his tiny form must have been overwhelming—but soon he started nibbling at a small patch of clover in the grass. I watched him munch contentedly for about ten minutes, and then curiosity overcame. I had to see if Bugs and Cocoa were going to get along.

Opening the door to the hutch, I anticipated Cocoa's reaction—would he be protective or aggressive towards a creature less than half his size? The rabbitry owner had told me Cocoa was a docile breed.

My idyllic vision quickly dissolved. Cocoa, after a hasty nudge of his brown wriggling nose to Bugs' gray wriggling nose, started chasing—as fast as he could—poor Bugs around the pen.

The bunnies had joined my animal circus.

That first day of both rabbits sharing the hutch was utter bedlam. The dogs, keyed to watch spring tension, their eyes lit up stimulant-unnaturally, badgered the hopping fur balls without cease. The foot-wide spot I'd left unblocked so the rabbits could see out was all my dogs and cats needed—they swarmed that spot as if the hutch was made of liver. I tried covering the spot but that didn't help, given that the cats could jump over the outer wall and my dogs were stimulated as much by scent as sight. Their interest would surely wane soon, I told myself. I couldn't house the dogs and cats inside all day, so I tried my best to ignore their misbehavior, and crouched down to get inside the three-foot-tall hutch yard with my rabbits, sitting on a small metal stool. They didn't seem to care much about me. Instead, they were intent on each other. Cocoa was establishing dominancy, and Bugs gamely tried to accept his situation.

Bunnies, cats, and dogs went through a week of assimilation boot camp before I noticed the first signs of waning interest in the cats. They seemed, sour-grapes-fox like, to indicate "I didn't want those rabbits anyway."

The dogs were a little slower to give up, but eventually they, too, settled down.

Then it was just my rabbits I watched.

I'd take breaks from my online teaching to make sure Cocoa wasn't harassing Bugs. Sometimes I shut Cocoa in the hutch—a roomy area, and the roof could be lifted back to allow fresh air to enter—while Bugs got the run of the hutch yard, and sometimes vice versa. Sometimes they appeared to be co-existing peacefully, and I felt a burst of pride that I'd pulled off a never-before-seen wild/domestic cohabitation. Other times Cocoa would pester Bugs, and I'd confine Cocoa for the day. Bugs would have been perfectly happy existing in peace, if Cocoa would let him.

When Cocoa was in an especially dominant mood, I'd bring Bugs back into the bathroom for a daylong time out. Eventually, they appeared to work out an uneasy détente.

≺: ≺: ≺:

What my rabbits needed was a good-sized pen. If I were a rabbit, I wouldn't want to live out my life in a small space. It was clear the hutch with its 4' x 7' "yard" wasn't going to cut it.

I couldn't wait to see my idea for a pen come to fruition. The first step was finding a rabbit pen contractor. Bob, a jack-of-all-trades who had mowed the lawn at the Fairbury house, said he'd take the job. I offered $30 per hour plus $60 per hour for skid loader work to level the ground. I gave him my general ideas; he agreed to build a pen that would look good, and gave me a list of supplies to pick up, including thirty landscaping bricks, six landscaping posts, hail screen, chicken wire, and latches for the door. Any other lumber we needed was available—collected by my father over the years—in our grain bin and corncrib.

We started work on the pen on a pleasantly sunny day in late May. Bob leveled a spot in our front yard between two huge shade-providing hackberry trees. The dense growth of branches on these fifty-footers would protect the rabbits from blazing July heat as well as shelter them from the onslaught of winter's snows.

Once he leveled the ground, we marked out the perimeters, 12' x 8', and started digging holes for the 10' posts at each corner. This was the hardest part of the day. Although the ground was fairly soft, digging a post hole to a depth of four feet takes dedicated effort.

During any hard job, the normal response is to gripe or to joke. I mostly joked. I was almost giddy with happiness; finally, I was working on a project that didn't involve rusty old junk. The only downside was Bob's history with rabbits, which was entirely about killing them for food.

I demanded to know how, in good conscience, he could chop the head off an innocent creature, adding "Rabbits are so sweet and tender!" I was referring to their demeanor.

I shuddered at his jovial reply, "Exactly! Rabbits are sweet and tender!"

If I'd had a choice, of course I wouldn't have hired a rabbit killer to build a rabbit pen, but as I've already indicated, most men in these parts see rabbits as prey.

I threatened to tell his hunting buddies, all of whom had killed their share of rabbits, that Bob had gone to the "other side" by building a deluxe "rabbit spa" in our yard, complete with landscaping bricks, to which he chortled, "Knock yourself out."

Bugs was hanging out in the bathroom while we built the pen, and I had moved Cocoa from the hutch, which we would shortly be moving into the pen, to a small cage on a nearby picnic table, where he could watch our progress. Cocoa's nonplussed stare at our labors spurred me to further joking while we positioned 2' x 4's across the top of the structure to make a roof frame. I pointed out that instead of working for "The Man" we were working for "The Bunny." Bob chortled again.

I soon noticed Bob's penchant for getting every surface on the pen level; his exactness impressed me. I continued the joking, musing that Cocoa was eyeing our efforts, thinking to himself, "It's off plumb."

"Tell Chocolate I'll show him what's plumb," Bob retorted.

"It's Cocoa."

"Whatever."

After four hours, the framework was up. The wood hutch from China, with its little enclosed yard, now sat at one end of the bigger pen, providing a kind of double protection. However, we hadn't yet stapled the hail screen on all four sides and top, nor had we made or installed the door.

We decided we'd done enough rabbit spa building for that day, and agreed to meet the next Monday to finish the job. I worried all weekend that Bob would call Monday morning, saying something had come up and he wasn't going to return.

He was a man of his word, though, and rolled into the yard at 9:30 a.m. Four hours later the pen was nearly complete, and I told Bob I'd handle the rest, asking before he left if he wanted me to create a web site advertising his services as "Rabbit Spa Builder to the Stars."

Stitching together the chicken wire ceiling to prevent animals from entering was the final step. I'd purchased a two-foot wide roll, and it took six strips to cover the top. I had to join five seams so my cats or other climbing animals that may stray into our yard wouldn't find any holes to shimmy through. I also secured the seams of the hail screen covering the sides of the pen with zip ties every foot or so to make sure there were no loose spots, and laid chair-seat-sized limestone rocks around the outer perimeter of the pen to prevent my dogs from digging their way in, as well as the rabbits from digging their way out.

The spot we'd built the pen on was bare dirt. I couldn't bear to see my bunnies hopping on dirt. The solution: carpet-square-size pieces of clover sod. Digging sod proved just as hard as digging fence postholes. Despite it being a cool day, sweat rolled off me. My hope was that the clover would quickly root and create a permanent ground cover in the pen, but alas, rabbits are diligent nibblers, and the clover carpet was gone in a month. I later covered the bare dirt with straw and brome hay.

First to go in was Cocoa. The moment I set him into his newly-expanded and improved home, he took off, kicking up his hind legs in a twist of joy that made me happy down to my bones.

Bugs, waiting patiently in the bathroom, was equally happy to find himself back on natural turf. After the not-so-successful pairing of the two bunnies in the small hutch yard, I wondered if the significantly bigger yard would solve the problem. The short answer: No. It wasn't long before Cocoa tried to establish dominance by mounting poor Bugs, who was not enthused by this development, but didn't know how to fight back, except by darting away.

Was I two pints shy of a quart, working so hard to please rabbits? My will to see the two get along persisted. I knew they would work out an arrangement in their new living quarters. I wouldn't rest until they did.

One morning, at 1 a.m., in the midst of a torrential downpour, I ran to the hutch to shut its roof. Cocoa and Bugs sat huddled, side by side, so close you couldn't put a finger between them, trying to stay dry under the ramp leading to the hutch. While the rain lashed as I closed the roof and placed a towel inside to soak up the puddled water, I marveled at their quiet acceptance—caught in a pickle, Cocoa was a perfect gentleman, willing to sit quietly with his wild counterpart to wait out the storm.

$\mathscr{J}$UNE

$\mathscr{B}$UGS DISCOVERS DELICACIES

Spring reached its zenith, and the delectation of early summer usurped. Roses burgeoned and berries ripened. Cocoa settled down and treated Bugs peaceably for a full week after the huddled-together-in-the-rain episode.

His good behavior didn't last. Cocoa's harassment of Bugs went something like this: Bugs would be minding his own business, contentedly munching on a pile of fresh clover in a corner of the pen. Cocoa, in another corner of the pen, kept Bugs in his eye line while distractedly crunching down a few strands of his own clover pile, nefarious plans bubbling in his hormone-addled brain. Those large brown eyes of his would have seemed the picture of innocence had he been alone in the pen, but with what he saw as a mate in sight, his gaze appeared baleful, verging on malevolence. Or maybe it was just ardency. Half a clover stem hanging from his mouth, Cocoa commenced his approach to the hapless Bugs, the first few hops cagily tentative, sussing out Bugs' reaction. Bugs, ever alert, stood guard, directly facing Cocoa and alternately pressing his front paws into the ground, as if kneading. This signaled his readiness to move. Undeterred, Cocoa continued towards Bugs, a small grunt accompanying each hop. Once Cocoa encroached too far into Bugs' space—a two-foot circumference—Bugs darted away in a quicksilver flash of fur to the other side of the pen. Then the chase was on. My protests of "Stop it, Cocoa!" went unheeded.

To his credit, though, Bugs began showing an admirable scrappiness. In the middle of one chase, he decided he would have no more of Cocoa's unnatural advances; he turned on a dime, and boxed kangaroo-style at Cocoa's face, until Cocoa tired of the game and went back to munching clover.

I knew Bugs would appreciate a space he could claim as his own, so I found a 2' x 2' wooden box and used a keyhole saw to cut a small entrance hole in one end, just big enough for him to squiggle through, but barring Cocoa. Bugs was half the size of three-pound Cocoa.

Bugs slept in his box during the day; Cocoa slept in the hutch. At twilight, both rabbits displayed their crepuscular nature and hopped around the pen together. Little Bugs' placid "live and let live" nature endeared, while Cocoa's bullying disturbed.

Bugs always had his little box to retreat to, which Cocoa couldn't infiltrate, so I didn't worry about his safety. I kept telling myself Cocoa was a docile breed and couldn't ever hurt Bugs.

The tame-and-wild setup hiccupped along. Then, one day I noticed Cocoa gnawing at the edge of Bug's wooden box. New to rabbit keeping, I wasn't keen to their prodigious gnawing power, so I didn't think much of it. A couple of days later, the entrance hole to Bugs' box had grown, and when I looked in, Cocoa sat triumphantly in Bugs' spot. I could have sworn Cocoa was gloating, while Bugs, thumping his hind leg in warning outside *his* box, was positively *glaring* at Cocoa, a thin crescent of white showing above his irises.

Another layer crumbled from my visions of gentle, peace-loving rabbits coexisting in everlasting harmony. Turns out, I read online, two male rabbits will fight to the death in some cases. Now what? Not arriving at any long-term fix, I made do with a temporary one, and started keeping Cocoa in the hutch with the door to the "yard" closed, leaving the rest of the pen to Bugs. Maybe these restrictions to his freedom would teach him to leave Bugs alone, I reasoned. Cocoa made his displeasure with confinement clear by gnawing on the door to the hutch, and scrabbling at the hail screen with his front paws. I realized what I really needed was another pen for Cocoa, but I also rationalized I shouldn't have to give in to Cocoa's waywardness so soon after building a more than adequate pen for two rabbits. I knew Bugs could be a feisty rabbit if required, and Cocoa seemed too docile to seriously hurt him. I found another hideout box for Bugs with a hole too small for Cocoa, nailed some tin around the hole to prevent his chewing the hole bigger, and after a week, opened the door to the hutch to let Cocoa run free in the pen with Bugs again.

I told myself any day now Cocoa would realize mating with Bugs was futile, and leave him alone.

Good luck with that thinking, nature soon replied. A few days after Cocoa's penetration of Bugs' box, I noticed tufts of Bugs' fur in the hutch, evidence of the two scrapping. I considered getting Cocoa neutered, but some quick online research showed this wasn't a foolproof method to ending his rabbity horniness. The battle continued. I saw, by way of my two rabbits, why there would never be peace in the world.

The farmyard, after the auctions, was still dotted with detritus to clean up, which I worked on sporadically between my online teaching, animal care, and the new project I instigated: saving our 75-year-old barn. I'd witnessed the barn deteriorate slowly over the last forty years; half the shingles had peeled off or fallen through, leaving the roof a sad patchwork that would be doomed, within a couple of years, to complete ruin unless fixed soon. Rick, the guy who'd helped me prepare for the farmyard auctions and clean out the Fairbury house, recommended a roofing crew, and they were able to start the project soon after I called them. Prep work had to be completed before the roofing started; Rick and I cleared out a rabble of rotten lumber, scarred wooden doors, rusted-out lawn-mowers, and other assorted junk from the south stalls of the barn. Those stalls had once been inhabited by my childhood dream—a pony—but the pony didn't like to be ridden, and my father didn't have the patience for horses, so he was sold to a local who used him to pull carts in parades. The stalls had since been used as prime real estate for dad's farm auction finds. I cussed the grimy sweat that coated me during the weekend of clearing out those stalls, reminiscent of the thirty-plus years of dust and grime I'd encoun-tered sorting auction items in the big implement shed. And, sever-al live trees in the way of the roofers had to be felled and the wood cut into fireplace-size logs. However, the barn project constituted a major shift in the dynamics of our farm: I was no longer simply clearing out junk; I was actively saving a historic structure that deserved to live. I envisioned that barn, newly roofed and painted, becoming an impressive focal point.

The crew started replacing joists in early June. I helped when I could, carrying lumber and steel panels. They screwed down the last piece of roof flashing on June 21. Our weathered barn now sported a dark green tin roof.

The crowning touch: A huge weather vane I'd found online, featuring a gold eagle with outstretched wings, stood proudly at the westernmost ridge. That symbol of freedom was my stamp. I saw myself living here for the rest of my life, improving the farm year by year, maybe even to showplace status.

I started planning the painting of the barn, to start in September.

Nearly every day, usually in the cool of the evening, I'd sit on a small metal stool I kept in the corner of the pen, and observe Cocoa and Bugs. Bugs appeared to be fully acclimated to his semi-domestic life. I respected his wild nature and didn't try to pick him up or hold him—he wouldn't have let me anyway—but on occasion, I would reach out my index finger after pouring his morning ration of alfalfa pellets and sunflower seeds in his dish, and he would let me stroke his forehead or shoulders once or twice before he got nervy and darted away. He always took treats gently and politely from my fingers. I'd tell him "What a good rabbit," marvel at his blueberry-size black-brown eyes, and wonder what went on in his mind.

Mulberry trees along the side of our driveway provide a rare treat during June. Every year while growing up, I'd note their progress as I walked to retrieve the mail. In late April the catkin-like flowers would appear, which soon developed at the base into green caterpillary-spiked berries. During May, I'd forget about the berries' progress. Then, in early to mid-June, during a bright sunny morning walk to the mailbox, I'd suddenly notice the tree's branches polka-dotted with black, a perfect concupiscence of nature. I'd set the mail down and pick the berries to my heart's content, fingers stained blackish-purple with the delectable juice.

This year, seeing mulberries on a list of rabbit-preferred fruit treats I found online, I picked a few for Bugs and Cocoa. Cocoa's I placed in a small dish for him to find. Then I found a pat of brome hay to sit on and held a berry for Bugs to taste. He approached in his usual fashion, hesitantly, planting his hind feet and elongating the back of his body while stretching his neck towards me, in order to keep his distance. Eventually, though, curiosity won out: he snuffled delicately at his first mulberry, then bit at it with relish and chewed methodically, savoring the sweetness. After twenty seconds or so, his thin V-shaped tongue, stained light purple, flicked out in one side of his mouth, then the other. He eagerly took another mul-berry from me, again chewing thoroughly before repeating the tongue-flicking, his tongue a darker purple this time. I could have watched this all day, but I'd read in every rabbit care guide to be cautious when giving new treats—to give only a small amount to avoid digestion problems—so Bugs had to be content with three mulberries. For a couple of weeks, though, he was treated every other day with three or four of the small gems. I later offered him raspberries and blackberries from the bushes near my vegetable garden; he loved these too. The blackberries' seeds sounded like gravel crunching in his mouth as he chewed. Watching him eagerly devour fresh fruits and vegetable snacks from my garden, I wondered if any other wild rabbit lived as kingly as little Bugs, all his needs met daily, with assurance against becoming prey.

I still mused, on occasion, about Bugs' sister. She would probably be slightly larger than Bugs; female cottontails grow larger than males. Despite not dining on alfalfa pellets, fruit, vegetable, and nut treats Bugs enjoyed, I imagined she found all kinds of protein-rich wild seeds, and maybe even berries, to supplement her grass and clover diet. Rabbits will even eat insects on occasion, if hungry enough.

Bugs' sister's days were numbered by the harsh realities of nature's pecking order, but I believe God may see fit to give greater fullness of being to those creatures who don't remain on the earth long. They must know, with some wisdom we can't fathom, that they are vulnerable, or they wouldn't know to run from danger. That's why every day that passed made the idea of releasing Bugs harder—he was becoming less and less fearful of my animals peering at him from outside his pen; it followed that his guard may be too relaxed in the wild.

Despite being at the low end of the food chain, could it be rabbits in the wild are content until the moment their number comes up? And, in the jaws of a predator, do they mercifully lose consciousness so their death isn't painful?

Questions like those ran through my mind in the still moments before sleep came. I also thought about my father's last hours on earth, alone at the age of 81 in a hospital room on a cold dark December night, bleeding internally from an old hernia that re-ruptured while cleaning out a room in the basement after a plumbing leak. Mom sat in the waiting room all night, and when she visited him in the morning, true to his football coach and Navy Commander demeanor, there was no "I love you" or even an acknowledgement that he may be dying. He ordered her to leave. His last words to her were incongruously trivial—a reminder of grocery items to buy, ending with "don't forget bananas."

He'd purchased our farm in the early 1970s near the homestead where he grew up because, as he said, it was the best place to raise kids. An ambitious farmer, at one time he owned over one thousand acres, yet he lacked the crucial quality any farmer needs: patience. I remember his booming, "I have sixteen thousand things on my mind!" when stressed. My brother and I could never figure out why he lighted on sixteen thousand. His other favorite was "You wonder why I'm angry," signaling his sour disappointment with the vagaries of farming, and, as I later learned, money problems. He did not tolerate human foibles in others or in himself.

I was the only family member to sob audibly as his casket was lowered into its final resting spot, but they were sobs of regret for what never was. On several occasions during the last years of his life, when I'd come to visit for a few days and the visit was, as usual, strained, he'd pull up a chair on the front porch and sit there quietly as I was getting ready to leave, telling me he'd checked the oil in my vehicle, and it was fine. I think he was waiting for me to pull up a chair and talk. Maybe we'd have that final talk of reconciliation. But we never did.

With the work Dad had left for me, I didn't have much time to ruminate on missed opportunities, but they shadowed my mind, especially at night when all was quiet. Solace came in doing what needed to be done to get the farm back into shape.

Even more solace came in Bugs' survival.

Now that he was the length of my hand, a young adult, I realized keeping Bugs captive excluded his natural proclivity to mate. In subverting nature, was I asking for trouble? We may think we can tame nature, but nature always wins. Long after humans are gone from the planet, the world of nature will remain.

As if in answer to my question, a bad surprise greeted me one morning: I opened the front door and found lying on the door-mat a half-grown and half-eaten rabbit. A tidal wave of shock and anger surged that I'd felt only once before, upon seeing a favorite kitten left dead on our porch by a stray dog. For an instant, I thought one of my cats had entered the hutch, cat-burglar style, through some unsecured spot, and killed Bugs. I immediately looked towards the pen and there Bugs stood. Safe. Stock-still in the morning light.

Despite my relief, I rued the death of a creature that may have suffered before exiting the world. Cussing my cats for their bloodthirsty ways, I picked up the remains of the dead rabbit and found a decent place to bury him.

June was befouled—courtesy of my predatory felines—by a total of three dead-rabbit-on-the-porch reminders of nature's ruthless ways. One was fully intact, and two were half-eaten, deposited with what I read as a malicious note of "This is what we'd do to Bugs, if only we could." My cats were toying with me.

I buried each of those unlucky rabbits near the redbud tree on the west side of our yard. None of the cats were in attendance at these makeshift funerals. They slept the sleep of the innocent on the porch, their slitted eyes barely acknowledging my "Rabbit killers!" admonition as I passed by them to return the burial spade to the shed.

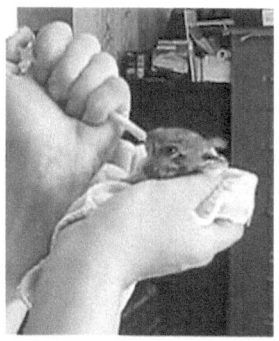

Feeding Bugs formula at two weeks

Bugs eating greens at three weeks

Bugs in his hutch at eight weeks

Duane, Opie, and Sophie: "What's in there?"

More curiosity from Othello, Duane, Opie, and Rocky

It's not a pen, it's a "deluxe rabbit environment"

Back view of rabbit environment

The "cabana" hutch outfitted with air-conditioner

Bugs at about five months

Bugs indoors

A fine-looking rabbit

Bugs' first mulberries

Cocoa and Bugs in hutch

Bugs and Cocoa after separation

$\mathcal{J}$ULY

$\mathcal{A}$IR-CONDITIONED
RABBITS?

True to form, June enacted its yearly about-face, morphing from temperate to sweltering. The seventh month in our humid-continental grass biome climate is not lucky; rather, July waxes tropically torpid. Much of my vegetable garden matures during this month, and I tend it carefully. Otherwise, my animals and I spend the bulk of July in the air-conditioned indoors.

July of 2012 began in particularly hellish fashion, with temperatures reaching 100 and above, 75-100% humidity, and demonic dew points climbing to an unbearable 70 or higher on some days. Rabbits have no way to sweat, and they don't pant like dogs, making them extra vulnerable to heat stroke. The owner of the rabbitry where I first met Cocoa told me to freeze water in a two-liter bottle for him to lie by on hot days. I tried the frozen-water-bottle cooling system for both Cocoa and Bugs on a few of the hotter days of June, but all the predictions were for miserably hot and humid conditions ahead, and I knew ice bottles weren't going to be enough. The deep shade of the two hackberries over their pen helped, but the trees didn't block the stifling humidity.

All six of my dogs and cats stayed inside in air-conditioned comfort on hot days. My rabbits were now part of my animal family and needed similar care. The first day the temperature reached 95 and the dew point 70—July 1, in fact—I wasted no time retrieving Cocoa's indoor cage—given to me by Jim, the guy who'd helped burn piles of unsaleable junk before the auction, who found it in a pile of giveaway junk on a street near his home. At two-by-three feet, it wasn't huge, but it was roomy enough for a day inside; Cocoa had stayed in the cage while watching Bob and I build his pen, and didn't appear to mind the close quarters. I lined the bottom with newspaper and wood shavings, and added a water bowl and feed bowl. Dogs wag their tails, cats purr, but rabbits flop down on their side and lie "bathing suit style" (stretched out like a model posing for the camera) to show contentment. Soon after I brought him indoors, Cocoa flopped on his side, cooling his paws, only ten feet from where I worked on my laptop. I was content that he was content.

I didn't forget Bugs. He revisited his old haunt the master bathroom on the first blistering hot days of July. Catching him created a problem, though. I had to wait until he was in the hutch, or try to lure him there with treats, then hold a cat carrier directly in front of the hutch doorway with one hand, while reaching my other hand into his space; he would then scuttle out of the hutch and into the carrier. Now that he was in his fourth month and showing wilder tendencies, capturing him was stressful for him and me, but Bugs seemed content to hang out in the blissfully-cool bathroom during the heat of the day. I'd visit him every few hours to say "hi" or offer him an apple or banana slice.

During Cocoa's first "indoor afternoon," each cat took turns sitting on top of his cage, and my poodle Opie circled the cage for a good half hour, ears pointed, earnestly whining. As the long hot summer days dragged on, the fun I experienced in Cocoa's indoor visits lessened, and turned to amazement at the volume of his poop that accumulated, even in a single day. Despite our neighbor girl Grace dubbing the poop pellets "Cocoa Puffs," those pellets were copious and relentless. They are superior fertilizer, though. My Morden Blush roses especially love rabbit poop, exhibited by lush garlands of white-pink blooms.

To allow them exercise, I'd put Cocoa and Bugs back in their outdoor pen after it cooled to below 75 degrees in the evenings. Some evenings it never cooled, and they stayed in all night.

❧ ❧ ❧

A final straw, so to speak, ended bringing the rabbits indoors on hot days. I ran out of wood shavings for Cocoa's indoor cage, and lined his cage with fresh straw from a bale I'd purchased from a nearby farmer. Seemed fine, albeit my mother didn't like straw poking out of the cage onto the carpeted bedroom floor. To appease her, I placed the cage inside a cardboard carton with four-inch sides so Cocoa's periodic shuffling wouldn't cause the straw to litter the carpet. I didn't account for what might be *in* the straw, though. One morning I woke with two small lumps about an inch below either eye. At first, the spots didn't seem too bad, although they itched a little. I was used to picking ticks off me by the dozens from April through August, and had grown immune to bug bites—getting used to bugs is a requirement of country living.

By the end of the day, the two spots had swelled ominously, and I felt headachy and tired. I begged out of going to dinner with relatives that night, took a Benadryl, swabbed calamine lotion on the bites, and went to bed.

I woke with eyes puffed like campfire marshmallows, and a stinging itch on both cheeks that, if bottled, could serve as a masterful device of torture. I tried ice packs on my face and took more antihistamine, reasoning that the poison would dissipate within a day or two. Knowing what constituted serious injuries on a farm, I hesitated going to a doctor for something so minor.

By the next day, I was in utter agony. My eyes looked like a boxer's after being knocked out, minus the bruises. Mom, knowing my resistance to doctors, knew any attempt on her part to get me to go would be futile. My pain-riddled brain prevented my putting two and two together: the straw contained the spider that bit me. Cocoa was still in his cage, lounging comfortably in that straw. Apparently, the spider that bit me didn't like rabbit flesh, as I saw no swollen areas on him.

By day four, the skin around my eyes and the entire upper half of my face felt like it was cracking and peeling away. I slathered on Vitamin E oil and pressed frozen washrags and ice packs against the swelling, none of which helped much. Finally, I broke down and while Mom was out getting groceries, I drove myself to a nearby clinic, where steroids were prescribed to get me over the worst of the next few days.

Once the swelling abated, I focused on finding a climate-control solution for Bugs and Cocoa. Both were growing increasingly restless being cooped up indoors.

What would I need to stay cool if I were a rabbit? Why, an air conditioner! The hunt began. Online shopping over the past ten years had become second nature to me—there was no item so obscure I couldn't find it, and hunting for the best price was part of the fun. Many of my purchases were gourmet food products I'd seen on the Food Network. Finding brown jasmine rice was easy, so was white truffle oil. Then there were the obscure kitchen gadgets, like French presses and mandolins. But try searching "mini air conditioner"—you won't get many results. I weeded through a lot of descriptions of small "air cooler" units for $25-50 that would fit inside the hutch, some that required periodic addition of cold water. Reviews indicated these units were less than effective. I needed a unit that would effectively cool a space neither airtight nor insulated.

I upped the ante and decided my rabbits needed a bona fide Freon-containing small-room air conditioner. I found a $99 model at Wal-mart online. Sold! It arrived two days later, on a sweltering 100-degree day at the end of the first week of July. I couldn't wait to get it set up and running to see if the bunnies liked it. I figured if the stars aligned fortuitously, the cool environment would create such a happy Cocoa, he would behave and quit trying to mount Bugs while they shared the luxury of their hutch.

An old wood nightstand held the A/C unit, placed at the hutch's side door, with the electric cord running up through the chicken-wire ceiling of the pen, connected to a heavy-duty extension cord running from the outlet outside our front door.

In no time, the rabbits were luxuriating in their "cabana hutch" with a prayers-answered bonus: no harassment of Bugs by Cocoa, at least that I could see. Setting the dial on "low cool" between the three and four setting produced a cool but not cold hutch interior.

"You know that's going to run the electric bill up," mom said, predictably.

"*I* pay the electric bill!" I retorted. "Plus, it's an energy-efficient unit. You won't even notice."

The first several days the unit ran, I checked on the hutch every couple of hours. The ever-growing but still compactly-sized Bugs usually huddled in his favorite spot in the nesting box at the back of the hutch, cool as a cucumber, with Cocoa preferring to sit near the hutch entrance. I sentimentally imagined a look of gratitude in their eyes, knowing it was ridiculous but wanting to believe they fully appreciated my largesse. Living in an area of the U.S. where such extravagances for animals are not the norm, I knew I was ripe for an eccentric label by neighbors, but I'd long ago determined I would never live to please people. As long as my animals loved me, I was content.

Cocoa's penchant for sitting near the hutch entrance, seemingly harmless at first, slowly revealed itself as an insidious way to torment Bugs, who needed to leave the hutch to eat, drink, and defecate. A picture I took of the two in air-conditioned bliss,

Cocoa in the foreground, his brown eyes glowing red from the camera's flash, Bugs sitting meekly in the background, spurred an observant comment from my ex Kelley, who was still keeping track of "dat ode Bugs" as he playfully called him: "Did you notice Cocoa has an *evil* look? I think he's laying for poor Bugs." Kelley had never seen Bugs face to face, yet he was as concerned for his safety as I was. I didn't see any evidence of outright attack by Cocoa, however, and let the situation ride.

The rabbits' air-conditioner stayed on nearly all day and night the entire month, while I kept a watchful eye on Cocoa's maneuvers around Bugs. At least my bunnies weren't sweltering in what was later determined the hottest July on record nationwide. I watched the green beans and tomatoes I'd lovingly tended in May and June dry to shreds in the devil's oven with a little less regret because my newest animal additions were thriving.

Well before the end of July, I started thinking about what my rabbits would need to stay comfortable during the equally extreme days of January and February.

AUGUST

A PEN DIVIDED

The long hot days of summer persisted. I hadn't seen any tufts of fur in the pen, and thought Cocoa had finally given up his "love that dare not speak its name" pursuit of Bugs. But you know what they say about idle hands … or, in this case, idle rabbits. The tide-turning moment came in early August, when I discovered poor Bugs' shoulders scraped raw, bleeding in two dime-sized patches, an injury I knew was the naughty Cocoa's doing.

The best I could figure is Cocoa had mounted Bugs, grabbing hold of his shoulders with his paws or maybe his teeth, to hold him. Bugs would have fought to free himself, and in so doing, Cocoa's grip raked him raw. My brother from California was visiting, and I discovered Bugs' injury the morning we were headed to Kansas City for his return flight. We still had a few minutes. I rushed to find a cat carrier to retrieve Bugs, and was able to get him quickly into the carrier with an apple slice. Once inside the house, I took him to his old haunt the master bathroom, and with gloved hands carefully reached for him inside the carrier, anticipating that this direct forcible handling, something I never did otherwise, may produce a frightened bite from him. My brother held a bottle of hydrogen peroxide, ready to pour—it would clean the wound painlessly. I scooped Bugs out of the carrier and quickly onto the bathroom counter he'd once slept on as a baby, and for the brief second he allowed himself to be held before leaping away like the wild creature he most emphatically is, the germ-killing hydrogen peroxide reached its target, sizzling on the raw wounds. I quickly poured Bugs some pellets and found him a water dish, and locked the door to the bathroom, letting Mom know what happened so she'd not open the door inadvertently and let Bugs out, a potential disaster I took extra precaution against by tacking a hastily scrawled sign on the door as well: "Rabbit Inside. Keep Door Shut!"

Despite our rush to get going, I could tell she had grown fonder of Bugs by her reaction of "What?! How bad is it?"

I told her he'd be okay, and that I'd explain more when I got home.

The wild-and-tame vision ended with this injury. Bugs' wounds healed fine within a few days, but I couldn't take any more chances. I called the rabbitry to see if they'd take Cocoa back. Although I'd grown fond of Cocoa, I had to protect Bugs. The breeders were overloaded with their own problems keeping their herd of rabbits cool during the record heat and couldn't deal with another. Once again, my father's junk came in handy.

I found one of his hoarded doors, hail screen framed by heavy wood. Set lengthwise in the middle of the pen and secured with two fence posts and wire, it served as a great divider. Cocoa, the offender, was given the side of the pen without the hutch, while Bugs, the underdog—and a sweet little non-trouble-causing-rabbit besides—was rewarded with the side of the pen that allowed full and unimpeded-by-Cocoa use of the air-conditioned cabana, or "rabbit mansion," as Grace, the same neighbor girl who called rabbit poop Cocoa Puffs, called it.

During the hottest days of August—not as bad as July but bad enough—I provided Cocoa with ice packs to lie against; I also ran a small room fan into a corner of his pen, and he was fine, albeit he doggedly scouted the pen divider for a weak spot he could squiggle through or under. For his part, Bugs took to gnawing the wood and sometimes the wire of the divider; I don't believe he wanted to mix with Cocoa, but he didn't like being restricted to half the pen. In fact, many would say, now that he was near full-grown, keeping him penned was against his nature and wrong. I'd also learned that keeping any wild animal captive is illegal without a license in Kansas. But our area was plagued with drought; I knew if I let Bugs go free, the extreme conditions would put him at a crippling disadvantage. He was used to daily feeding and watering. How would he find adequate sustenance? Would what he found be enough to keep him strong and healthy? I was feeding him a mix of freshly-picked brome grass and tender garden greens, alfalfa pellets with a sprinkling of groats, sunflower seeds, and dried fruit, plus the occasional mini carrot, banana slice, berries, and his favorite, a Fuji apple slice. Going from that rich and varied mix to an assortment of dried-up weeds could spell bad news.

I wrestled with my conscience many a time, telling myself I was denying his wild instincts in keeping him captive. Still, I could not bring myself to let him go. I didn't like the divided-pen solution, but it would have to do for now. My only other choice was to find another home for Cocoa, or build him his own pen.

My concerns around my "rabbees"—my new pet name for rabbits—had taken over; the two smallest beings of my menagerie had wriggled their way into prominence. I was now a confirmed "rabbit person," appreciating mightily the unassuming rabbit nature. My affinity for rabbits could stem from being a Rabbit in the Chinese astrological chart. Okay, maybe that stuff is hooey, but what's the harm? Those born in the year of the Rabbit are said to be calm peacemakers who avoid conflict at all costs; they also love comfort and are generally artistic. Sensitive to the point of being timid, Rabbit people tend to "hole up" away from the world to avoid being hurt. That was me, alright.

Once I'd delved into finding out more about wild rabbits, my rabbit googling became compulsive. Links telling how to prevent damage from rabbits outnumber three-to-one links about preserving rabbits. Rabbits are the only animal that are considered a pet, a food source, or a pest, depending on who you talk to.

My father saw wild rabbits as worthy of respect. His kindness towards animals was his best quality. I never forgot the night during my childhood he cried like a baby after accidentally running over a cat in our driveway. He even suggested the 4-H club presentation "Brush Piles for Bunnies" my brother gave when he was in the fifth grade. We did indeed build many brush piles for wild rabbits to hide in. Those who see wild rabbits as pests have perhaps lost a row of lettuce, tulips, or young fruit trees to their nibbling. Chicken wire fencing around a garden and a simple foot-high circle of hail screen around young tree trunks protects against that damage. I've never seen enough damage from rabbits to my garden or flowers to get upset. In fact, soon after finding Bugs, I planted lettuce and snap peas for the sole purpose of feeding him these special treats. There's no crunch like the crunch of a rabbit enjoying freshly-picked snow pea pods.

SEPTEMBER

SPIRIT GUIDE

Autumn approached, with its ageless attar of the ancient world. In Bugs' birthplace, section 26 of Farmington township, Republic County, Kansas—about seventy miles due east of the geographic center of the contiguous United States—white-tailed deer, raccoons, coyotes, bobcats, pheasant, wild turkey, hawk, quail, and all the other fauna surely welcomed the cooling temperatures. I caught glimpses of deer eating corn along the creek banks, a coyote darting in the fading brome, a covey of quail in the prairie grass.

The swallows leave during this month, some flying all the way to South America. The bittersweet end-of-summer air tells them when to leave every year, like clockwork.

Now that summer was ending, Bugs and Cocoa seemed more content. The fall semester was starting, and my days were a mix of paid work—grading essays and commenting in online class discussions—and unpaid work I did around the yard—mowing, weed-eating, and cleaning up debris left over from the auctions.

And, the barn painting project began. Painting a forty-foot-tall structure involves some planning and patience. I rented a "man-lift" at a cost of $450 for a weekend, to get Rick to the top of the gable on the front of the barn. The barn roofing crew had used the same machine; operating it looked easy enough, from a distance. It wasn't so easy with Rick and me at the controls. He bowed out on running the contraption early on, telling me, "I don't want it to be my fault if something goes wrong." *I* had to make it work, and somehow I did, but there were some tense moments when the legs didn't want to extend or retract like they were supposed to, and when it rolled away several feet after we forgot to block the tires when unhitching it. I vowed never to rent that particular piece of equipment again.

The barn painting took a good portion of the month. Instead of sweaty grime, I came in from long days of work with what appeared to be bloody splatters head to toe, from the barn-red paint.

When I had time, I could always head across the road with a pair of loppers to cut young cedars that grew like weeds in our forty-acre pasture, quickly reaching gargantuan size and overrunning the grass meant for our pasture renter's cows to graze. I'd hired two different tree cutters to fell the largest cedars during the past couple of months, but told them to leave the little trees—I'd get those myself.

There was always work to be done. Sometimes my preoccupation with the rabbits cut into other work I should have been doing—but how could I help that? They depended on me.

Spending time with my "rabbees" provided a meditation I craved. Cocoa didn't mind me holding and petting him, but I didn't do this often. His independent spirit made him appear aloof, which I liked about him. True to a rabbit's unassuming nature, he preferred seeing activity near his pen rather than being the center of activity. Despite his aloofness, I wanted to see how Cocoa might adapt to becoming a "free range" house rabbit, and let him hop around on my bed for five minutes one evening. All seemed well—my dog Opie sniffed at him but didn't lunge. Maybe I could welcome Cocoa to hop around on my bed more often, I thought. Just then, Cocoa froze, unnaturally still, and a yellowish-white puddle of urine grew like an evil flower beneath him. That was the end of Cocoa on the bed. I'd heard rabbits could be litter box trained, but I didn't relish the thought of attempting this project.

Bugs' usual interaction with me, when I entered the pen each day to feed and water him, was to stretch out his neck towards my hand, then touch his nose to my finger. "Good morning, Bugs!" I'd chirp, "How's the best rabbit that ever was?" He'd turn his head towards me—he knew his name. "Run and jump! Dance and sing!" I chanted, while his long ears twisted curiously. My other animals made me happy, but Bugs' acceptance was a rare prize. He'd grown used to my bringing special treats for him, and always checked my hand for apple or banana slices, mini carrots, or pea pods.

Our neighbor Ledona told me her daughter, years ago, had tamed a wild rabbit to the point she could carry him around. She must have spent a lot of time with that rabbit. I averaged a couple of hours a week sitting in the pen with Bugs, watching him eat and hop. On rare occasions, I was able to stroke his head or shoulders with a single finger. Only once did he let me stroke his back for *several* seconds, and I felt his sinewy fully-formed muscles under his sleek fur. Petting a wild rabbit is like eating truffles—you never forget the exquisiteness. Part of me wanted to be able to carry him around like a pet; then again, his elusiveness was part of his charm. And, trying to fully tame him would counter his natural instincts.

So, I was content to sit in the pen and watch Bugs from a foot or two distance. The chaotic state of the world, with its constant news of imminent wars and the downturn of the economy, fell away as I focused on his beauty. I counted nine separate colors in his fur: black, umber, sienna, bronze, gray, tan, buff, cream, and white. There were probably more. These colors mixed cleverly in a ticked pattern throughout his coat, making Bugs difficult to spot, sometimes even when he stood or lay in the open areas of his pen. His head had grown to the size of a child's fist, with those soulful eyes protruding on either side. How had they grown from tapioca-size to large-blueberry size so fast?

Variation within the cottontail genus is astounding. Sixteen subgenera of cottontails inhabit our planet. Some are rarely seen, others, like the Eastern cottontail (Bugs' subgenus) are ubiquitous. I wish I could see all the North American varieties close up—the New England cottontail, Mexican cottontail, Desert cottontail, Mountain cottontail, Manzano Mountain cottontail, Appalachian cottontail, the Swamp rabbit, Marsh rabbit, and the uniquely named Robust cottontail, indigenous to a small slice of territory in southwest Texas. Even more amazing is that each rabbit within its subgenus is unique as a snowflake: If I had to pick Bugs out of a lineup of other Eastern cottontails, I'd know him. His extra-large eyes, distinctive black spot the size of a shirt button in the middle of his starboard side, and his modesty about his cotton tail—he didn't fluff it up when hopping around the pen, but left it neatly tucked under—would identify him. Sometimes I wondered if he had much of a cotton puff under his scut, or hindquarters. I mused that maybe one day I'd see him speed away full blast, free, and I'd admire his speed, agility, and that white tail with a hearty "Excellent cottontail!"

Bugs' grooming routine was as fastidious as a cat's. After consuming his fill of greens and treats, he'd rise on his haunches, raise his paws to his face in a kind of prayer-stance, and lick his paws. Then, he'd use his wet paws to swipe his face, first one side, then the other, several times. Moving to his chest, he'd turn his head downward to lick. After his face and chest, he moved to his shoulders, turning his head to lick each in turn. Then, he'd lick his paws again and pull his ears down through his paws to get them clean. Finally, he'd work on his hindquarters, turning his head back to lick the fur on his haunches. His cleaning routine stayed pretty much the same and often took a good five minutes.

Sometimes he'd be grooming himself when I entered the pen to give him a treat, and I learned firsthand a strange fact: because a rabbit's eyes are on either side of its head—to better see predators from both sides—they have a blind spot directly in front. I'd drop a mini carrot or apple slice right in front of Bugs' nose, and he wouldn't see it. When I dropped it to the left or right side of his head, he'd go right for the treat.

I constantly marveled at his politeness. There was no quick swipe and dash; when I offered him an apple slice from my hand, he'd sniff at the proffered treat its entire length, find a suitable spot of the white flesh to sink his teeth into, then assertively crunch down. Usually he took his first bite halfway up the slice—never from one end—and he showed the same technique with snap pea pods. Once he secured the treat, he'd take it to a spot a foot or two away, where he'd nibble a mouthful, then drop the slice and chew deliberately, with what I imagined to be a blissful stare. It took six or seven mouthfuls to devour a quarter-inch thick apple slice.

I wondered what Bugs' sister in the wild considered a delicacy—she'd undoubtedly found mulberries dropped from trees, and even the occasional fallen apple or pear. At six months old, she would be able to bear young. I read that female rabbits can conceive at three months, and reportedly, about fifteen percent of them do. Because the cottontail lives a truncated lifespan, the precociously early breeding makes sense. I like to think Bugs' sister didn't breed as a juvenile, though. I think she met a suitor in the wild, maybe sometime during this month. A male who found her would enact a strange courting ritual—first, he'd "dance" an approach. Bugs' sister would box at him when he got close, and both would jump straight up a couple of feet. Maybe to show excitement? Then, the male would do something very few species do during courtship: he would pee on her. Sometimes the female retaliated. Could the reason be to mark each other with their scent for easier locating later? After urinating on each other, they would then groom each other prior to "the deed."

≼: ≼: ≼:

The final week of September rolled around. Golden pears hung pendant-like in the old orchard across the road; I waited for them to reach just the right hue before picking as many as I could reach. The cattle who grazed that pasture loved those pears too, eating with relish the ones that fell to the ground. Late September always presented one or more perfect afternoons, when a cool breeze breathed through the tall prairie grasses, bob-whites and mourning doves sounded over distant swells of pasture, and a lone cricket chirped in the ripening pumpkins.

Before Bugs, I'd experienced nature's perfection while working in my garden, digging potatoes, weeding, clearing the spent growth for next year's garden. This autumn, with a brisk breeze whistling through the hail screen of the pen, I spent several perfect afternoons feeding Bugs and Cocoa hackberries, the BB-sized seeds of the tree of the same name. These seeds taste like dates. They fall freely in our yard, and a few would drop through the chicken-wire roof of the rabbit pen. One day I happened to see Bugs nibbling on one, and from then on, I started picking them off the ground and placing them in the rabbits' food dishes. Watching Bugs carefully select one, mull it around in his mouth for half a minute, then delicately drop the inedible inner seed back into the dish, made me laugh out loud. Bugs was so used to my sitting in his pen watching him eat, I could make all the noise I wanted—talking, singing, even shouting at my cats Boots and Othello when their play outside the pen got too rough— Bugs would sit there contentedly chewing, as if nothing in the world mattered except the morsel in his mouth.

By the end of September, Rick and I had adorned the front of the barn with two coats of oil paint, and each side with one coat. A rainy week cut into our painting, and we called it quits for the year, with plans to finish the side and back of the barn sometime in the next year. Although we weren't quite done, I counted the saving of our barn as a bright spot. Mom even told me, "Your father would be proud of you." He had talked about roofing the barn fifteen years earlier, but somehow it never happened. Now it stood as a focal point of our yard, bright red with a dark green roof. I called it our "Christmas barn." An artist friend said I should rent out the barn for weddings. The yard was still a long way from showplace status, but I was gaining on it.

In the way that knowledge comes only when we're ready for it, I learned while randomly clicking around online, about the Native American practice of selecting animals as totems or spirit guides. Many tribes believe an animal totem comes into one's life to teach a lesson necessary at that time. Native American religion is based on animism, the belief that all natural creatures and even entities like trees and rocks possess souls. And, some tribes recognize rabbits for their powers, including the Shawnee tribe, originating in the Great Plains of Oklahoma. Rabbits, in animal totemism, can signify moving through fear, living by one's wits, receiving hidden teachings and intuitive messages, quick thinking, strengthening intuition, and paradox.

My quick call to grow up and take charge after my father's death jibed with every one of the lessons a rabbit totem teaches. Coincidence? I'd lived on our farm a total of fifteen years during my childhood and my adult life, amongst thousands of cottontail rabbits, but had never before been gifted with an orphaned cottontail to foster. Bugs came only after my father's death. The quality I loved about my father—his admiration for animals wild or tame—manifested in my saving Bugs. Dad had never shot a wild rabbit that I know of; instead, he had tried to preserve them by providing cover and food. He'd told me long ago, when I asked why he left unharvested rows along the edge of the fields, "That's for wild animals."

You may find this strange, but in the reflective mood that autumn brings, I saw clearly Bugs was not just any wild rabbit. The twinkling I'd felt soon after finding him had grown to a flame of assurance. If I closed my eyes and listened deeply, I could hear the musical hum of the earth spinning, a holy song all wild creatures know.

$\mathcal{O}$ CTOBER

$\mathcal{F}$ IRST FROST

Bugs and Cocoa's outdoor life encompassed an infinitely vibrant reality. The door of their pen stood only twenty feet from our home's front door, yet they were in constant contact with nature. In all the outdoor videos I took of them, songs of birds and rustling leaves are prominent. Come dusk, though, Sophie's and Opie's barking at coyotes dominated. The coyotes' yips and wails traveled clearly and uncannily across pastures; I couldn't tell if the pack was a mile away or a football field away. The yips from a nest of pups, urgently high-pitched, seemed to come from all directions at once. Sophie's sonorous "roooof" and Opie's nagging "yaap," repeated without cease, became a nightly concert.

The ghostly whining of an old windmill wheel that needed oil, a half-mile directly south of the yard, often joined the eerie symphony. For some reason, the rusty squeak sounded particularly creepy during an October night, and I wondered if this sound kept the rabbits awake.

Punctuating this rural symphony was the dull thwack of ripe black walnuts hitting the tin roof of an old machine shed where we stored garden tools and our riding mower. That walnut tree had seen at least seventy-five summers and winters. My father, seasoned by the Depression, had habitually gathered black walnuts and stored them in barrels and buckets, I suppose in case of famine. I kept finding his walnut stashes around the yard as I cleaned up the place. I knew he'd dislike my cutting down several black walnut trees he'd planted twenty years earlier, but they stood beside an unused chicken coop with a falling-in roof and damaged foundation; I arranged to have the coop demolished, burned, and the foundation buried early in the month. There were many black walnut trees around the yard besides the five or six that had to come down, and a productive corn patch went into the fertile ground near the demolished coop. Black walnuts, although egregiously difficult to extract from the iron-hard shell, *would* provide sustenance in case of a famine, but I ensured we'd have more choices in sustenance by planting three English walnuts and a butternut tree behind the house in early October.

During the last year of his life, my mother told me, Dad had rigged a makeshift squirrel feeder with husked black walnuts laid out on screens supported by a couple of barrels. He'd stand at the kitchen window watching the squirrels gather their walnut loot. Although I set out birdseed and suet during the winter, I'd never thought to feed squirrels. More proof of my Dad's love for animals, even those passed over as negligible by most people. I knew he would have liked watching Bugs too.

Our first frost fell on the 10th, and it was a hard one. Despite reading that rabbits prefer cold weather, once nighttime temperatures approached freezing, I acted quickly to protect them. Bugs was now nearly Cocoa's size, albeit slimmer in form. A heat lamp seemed an inexpensive and effective solution. I found one at a local farm supply, with a red 250-watt bulb, and installed it on the divider door between the two pens, with an extension cord running twenty-five feet to the same outlet I'd used for the air-conditioner. The lamp sat about two and a half feet up from the ground, so the heat could reach both Cocoa's and Bug's side of the divider. Although this wasn't an ideal setup, it worked. A hay-lined box under the lamp provided a warm spot to rest, and I placed both their water dishes on top of their boxes, under the heat lamp, preventing the water from freezing.

I made one mistake. I forgot to tell my mother about the heat lamp. She had often mentioned her fear of fire destroying the house, having read about various fires in our rural area. I suppose she'd never seen a heat lamp before. The night I set up the heat lamp, I was in the middle of grading essays when my mom ran into my bedroom, screeching, "There's a fire in the rabbit pen!"

My reassurance that there was no fire, and that the heat lamp would not cause a fire, met with skepticism. To assuage her, I googled "heat lamp fires," expecting to find nothing, but it turns out there *were* some warning posts from people who hadn't carefully secured a heat lamp, resulting in its coming into contact with dry hay and starting a fire. These accidents were usually the result of larger animals like goats interfering with a lamp, but even so, I realized it wouldn't hurt to secure the heat lamp with several zip ties. Mom eyed the lamp warily for a couple of weeks before letting up on the comments.

The lamp was doing its job, too—I often saw Cocoa sitting still at the furthest edge of where its heat reached; he enjoyed the warmth it provided, and Bugs liked to hang out in his wood box directly below the lamp.

Bugs and Cocoa touched noses frequently through their screen-door divider. I guess that meant they didn't hate each other. Because they were now an equal size, I started thinking I should try one more time to see if they could share the pen together peaceably, but decided to wait for a warmer time of the year when I could observe them more carefully.

November/December

Bugs' First Winter

Soon, the nighttime low temperatures inched towards the single digits, and I wasn't satisfied that the heat lamp provided enough comfort nor adequate heat during a rainstorm or snowstorm. The wooden boxes under the lamps weren't sufficient shelter.

It was time to winterize Bugs' and Cocoa's sleeping quarters. First, I applied clear silicone caulking along all the seams of the roof and sides of the hutch where wind could penetrate. Next, a mattress-sized piece of heavy-duty plastic I found in the garage—one of Dad's squirreled-away items—came in handy. I covered the screen door of the hutch with a piece cut from the plastic, then insulated the nesting box, and added a layer of protection under the fold-back roof, which I left closed all the time now. I had to fold myself in half to reach under the nesting box, but after an hour or so of stapling and taping plastic, I was satisfied. The crate-sized heavy wooden box where Cocoa slept was solid, but I knew it could use more insulation, so I set the box atop several wooden deck tiles, then filled the space below with bubble wrap and pieces of Styrofoam. I then placed a carpet square on the floor of his box, then brome hay, and covered the box with several heavy old towels. Finally, I wrapped the entire box in a thick piece of tarp, tucked under the edges and secured all around with bricks for good measure.

The next task was finding some way to heat Bugs' hutch and Cocoa's shelter. The hutch was full of hay, so a space heater was out of the question. Time to google "pet heating pads." Although I've since seen these pads at our nearby farm supply store, I didn't know they existed until I found a few outlets selling them online. Two small animal heating pads were soon on their way, ordered from a pet store in New York. Installing these was easy—I placed the pad in Cocoa's box, found a piece of PVC to protect the part of the cord that extended out from the pad—although the cord was advertised as "metal covered" it didn't seem rabbit-proof. I then placed Bugs' pad in his hutch, with the cord running straight up out of the roof.

Voila, the rabbit shelters were now heated. Bugs was wary of his pad, and for awhile I thought he wasn't using it. Although it ran at a very low heat, I'd placed a towel on it to make it more comfortable, and for a week the towel appeared pristine, no fur or dirt on it. Then, one cold morning, when I fed him his pellets inside the hutch, as I was closing the door, Bugs positioned himself on top of the heated pad while he ate his food. He continued to do this every time I fed him. I couldn't tell exactly when Cocoa started using his pad; it was hidden inside his box, covered with tarp and secured with bricks, which I didn't often disturb, but the few times I lifted the box to check that the pad was working, I found fur on the pad. The $48 I paid for those heating pads was money well spent. They stayed plugged in the majority of the winter of 2012 and even into the chillier-than-normal spring of 2013, finally coming out of Bugs' hutch and Cocoa's box in April.

A true sign of winter was the drying up of the brome grass I'd been picking fresh for Bugs and Cocoa all spring, summer, and fall. Brome grass is a staple in any Central Plains area. I'd always seen it as a nuisance in our yard; each spring, seemingly overnight, brome went from manageable height to four-foot tall stands of thick, seedy stalks that were hard to mow and harbored chiggers, those nasty bugs that burrowed under the skin and created an itch like fire. Brome has a way of hiding cable and propane lines when using a weed-eater, and seemed to flourish especially well amidst the leftover junk that dotted our yard after the auctions, creating islands of tall grass here and there that bothered me. Now, I had two brome-eating machines in my rabbits, and I happily provided them all they could eat of the stuff, having read that rabbits do well on a diet of seventy-five percent hay or grass. Timothy hay is the promoted food for rabbits; I noticed online there are services that will send timothy hay "fresh to your door." I scoffed at that idea. Our yard produced feed as good as or better than timothy hay. Even after the first freeze in October, brome grass stayed green. However, by mid to late November the grass took on a brownish-green hue, and was harder to pull. The rabbits didn't go for it like they did the greener brome. Now I would have to figure out a solution to keeping them in greens through the winter. Despite seeing cold frames described and promoted in gardening books and sites that allowed one to grow fresh greens into the winter, I'd yet to make one. The rabbits could eat baled dry brome grass, but it wasn't the same as fresh.

The first big snow was coming, and it would cover the brome. Still, I didn't get a cold frame built. My attention turned instead to providing a drier pen during the winter. While rabbits don't seem to particularly mind snow, I didn't want six to eight inches of the stuff in my rabbits' pen. Not only would they find it harder hopping through the mass; I would have a harder time feeding and watering them. While sorting items in the huge machine shed before the auctions, I had come across a huge heavy-duty Army-green canvas, folded up, weighing probably forty pounds, and had stashed it away in a corner of the shed, knowing it may come in handy someday. A few weeks before our first snow, I measured the canvas, then measured the pen. Nearly a perfect fit. It wasn't easy getting that canvas on top of the pen by myself, but the pen, solidly built, held it fine, and the canvas did its job—it even had large riveted holes all around, which I used to secure it to the pen with bungee cords. The morning after our first big snow, the top of the pen looked like a thickly-iced rectangle cake, and hardly any snow had sifted into the pen.

Anyone wondering why I made extra work for myself in covering the pen need only see the content bunnies in their sheltered space to understand. I fancied that Bugs and Cocoa knew they were a couple of pampered bunnies. I realize most city people wouldn't dream of keeping a domestic rabbit outdoors all year. However, Cocoa did come inside on the hottest days and coldest nights. Bugs, once full grown, did not like the confinement of the bathroom; he slept on his heating pad in his brome hay-insulated hutch, protected from the sharp sting of winter winds by our yard's surrounding cedar windbreak as well as the pine walls of his hutch. How was his sister in the wild surviving? I pictured her dug into a hole under the heavy, sheltering branches of a cedar, having eaten from a sparse choice of oak or elm twigs and wild plant growth that survived after frost covered the earth. At night while I listened to the winter winds howl, I pictured Bugs burrowed into his brome hay on top of his heating pad, his food and water right beside him. He was, if not fully content, at least not suffering. I hoped his sister wasn't suffering either.

On the second anniversary of my father's death, I decided to clean out the remaining clutter in the large machine shed; despite two auctions, there was still doo-dads and thingamajigs to be sorted through. I even came across an essay of mine dad had saved with other papers in a brown grocery bag, stuffed into a corner of the shed forty years earlier. My second-grade teacher had asked us to write about our personality. The first sentence, scrawled in my seven-year-old cursive: "I have a great love for animals."

There still wasn't room to park the Allis Chalmers 200 tractor, nor our Chevy pickup and Yukon in the shed. The tractor, a behemoth with a snow blade on the back, we'd kept to clear our driveway each winter. Once I got the hang of getting the blade set at the right height, it was a job I looked forward to, because it made me feel capable, self-sufficient.

Emptying "The Shed" was the last big cleanup job. I'd put it off until the barn restoration was done, and it loomed like death. It was too late now for the *American Pickers* to look around—95% of the valuables were sold and gone. Now it was *Hoarders* time. But even that crew would have shuddered and run for their Hazmat suits, complete with goggles. I toughed it out in jeans, flannel shirt, Carhartt jacket, gloves, and work boots. Jay, the guy who helped, I'd recruited from one of the auctions; I paid him $25 an hour; this wage kept him motivated until the job was done. We spent two weeks hauling scrap iron, sorting out the remaining saleable items, and carting endless wheelbarrow loads of pure trash, incinerated in dual bonfire piles that took several days to reduce to embers. Because it was near Christmas, and this was the last of the nasty tasks left to me, I bit my tongue at the billows of dust that rose when we dug into another corner of stacked wood, hubcaps, boxes of electrical connections, piles of broken-backed chairs, and stacks of empty soap boxes and rusted coffee cans. I continued to bite my tongue while stepping on tiny nails spilled out from the many cans of nails, screws, and other fasteners my father had stacked in haphazard rows along one wall side of the shed.

Those nails would have to be painstakingly picked up with a magnet before any vehicle could be parked in the shed.

I'm not much of a beer drinker, but the Bud I cracked open after carting the last wheelbarrow load of trash from that gape-mouthed shed, with snow under my boots and a bonfire before me, tasted like ambrosia.

JANUARY/FEBRUARY

ENDURANCE

The first snows of winter had come and gone, and the brome grass was completely frozen. My rabbits still wanted their greens every day, though. I tried sowing some grass seed in the huge planter that held my fig tree, brought in for the winter and placed in our laundry room, but the light from the east window wasn't sufficient, and it grew spindly and unsuitable as rabbit food.

The answer was a greenhouse, or at least a cold frame—a glass-enclosed outside growing area that can allow greens like lettuce and cabbage to grow all winter. Only so many projects could get done in a year, though, and I'd focused on the yard-beautifying projects. The cold frame or small greenhouse would have to wait until next year. To make do, I bought kale, parsley, snow pea pods, and romaine lettuce at the grocery as a supplement to Bugs' and Cocoa's daily alfalfa pellets and baled brome hay. At first, they seemed hesitant about the store-bought greens. I wondered if they smelled residual pesticide. Ironically, finding organic produce at rural grocery stores is difficult. I made sure to soak the greens I bought for at least a half hour, and rinsed them well. After seeming indifferent about kale and romaine at first, the two soon warmed to their purchased greens. I often mixed in a couple of mini carrots, plus their favorites, apple and banana slices. Sometimes for fun during the long winter days I'd lay out a row of various snacks—an apple slice, banana slice, and mini carrot—to see which they'd go for first. Cocoa would go for the banana slice, while Bugs always went for the apple slice.

While snows blanketed our farm and prevented outdoor work, I continued my reading about rabbits, both online and in a book I found online and immediately ordered: *The Private Life of Rabbits* by R.M. Lockley, a real-life study of cottontails in Britain. Published in 1964, it's the most comprehensive study of wild rabbits that exists, and fully engaged my interest. Richard Adams used facts from Lockley's book for *Watership Down.*

The oddest fact that stood out in all my rabbit research, besides their peeing ritual during mating, is that rabbits practice coprophagia, or eating their own feces, as a way to gain better nutrition. They eat only their *soft* feces, which are green pellets coated with a gelatinous membrane, rather than the normal brown pellets they more often excrete. I've never saw Bugs or Cocoa eat their green-pelleted poop, and part of me doesn't want to see it. Then again, if I happened to witness the phenomenon, and if I could get over the gross factor, I would consider it a fascinating natural observation.

During the coldest nights, I'd bring Cocoa indoors; he seemed happy enough in his cage overnight. I piled even more brome hay in Bugs' hutch, with the heating pad in the middle and a towel covering it, so Bugs could snuggle. I made sure he had plenty of alfalfa pellets mixed with slightly more sunflower seeds than usual, plus a peanut or two for extra calories. Every time I poured Bugs' pellet/nut mixture into his small glass bowl, he went to work sniffing out the six or seven sunflower seeds and one or two peanuts first, fairly inhaling them—just like when he was a baby and ate the pink and green groats first.

In the wild, Bugs' sister would have seen a pile of alfalfa pellets and sunflower seeds as manna; instead, she was eating bark and twigs to keep her energy level up. This, along with constantly being forced to find dry, protected shelter made for grueling days and nights. Bugs' European cousins, who didn't have to deal with such harsh winters, were ahead of the game in burrowing underground. I hoped Bugs' sister had found a suitable abandoned hole in the side of a bank left by some previous creature, maybe a badger sett, and claimed it for her own during the worst of the winter, as I've read some rabbits do.

February dragged interminably. All six dogs and cats stayed inside on cold days and nights, and the house became an animal hotel. Perhaps because of latent guilt that the rabbits didn't have their own room in the "house hotel," I saw winter in an even harsher light. When the Weather Channel announced that

March 1 was the first day of "meteorological spring"—a fact I'd never before learned—a rush of relief washed over me.

I started tomato seeds in flats, and kept my eyes peeled for the yard's first wild lettuce leaves and dandelions—the ultimate organics to feed rabbits.

MARCH/APRIL 2013

FREEDOM

The days wheeled towards the anniversary of Bugs' adoption—March 22. During the past year, I'd managed two big farm auctions, helped sort and haul items from the Fairbury home for ten smaller auctions—and we'd sold the house to the second couple who looked at it, saved our seventy-five-year-old barn with a roof and paint, cleaned out "The Shed," tore down and buried an old chicken coop, and improved the look of the yard with fruit trees, various flowering bushes, and roses.

Tangible proof of progress came during the first spring mowing of the year, when I didn't have to worry about hitting iron scrap hidden in the grass—those pesky items had been picked up and hauled away. That simple fact made me feel in control of a yard that a year earlier had been in disheartening disarray. Since the previous spring, the islands of grass-hidden junk in our yard had reduced from thirteen to four.

The symbol of my resolve to create a farmyard anyone would be proud of was the weather vane that stood high atop the peak of the barn roof. Every time I gazed at that golden eagle with its outstretched wings, I felt like flying myself.

I don't think the dead see us—they are far beyond our earthly worries—but I found myself wondering what Dad would say about my work. I imagined a kind of grudging pride. Then I imagined him wanting to make one last glory pile of the straggling bits of his junk collection, including that kitchen sink I'd hidden away before the first auction.

Dad had unwittingly let me prove myself. The earnings from the auctions were enough to give Mom a cushion in her final years.

Best of all, I was given the gift of Bugs.

Almost every night now, in the still quiet moments before sleep, an answer was forming, about what I needed to do to make Bugs happy, as he'd made me happy. He needed to be free. Free to find his own wild lettuce, dandelions, sorrel, and plantain. Free to find his own shelter under a brush pile or tree root. Free to hop as far as he pleased. Free to find a female. I doubted Sophie or my little dog Opie would bother Bugs if I set him free, and something told me he'd hang around the yard. A few times I'd opened the door to his pen while he stood by the open door, and he could have bolted, yet he never did. I surmised his natural peace-loving nature made him shy, unwilling to leave the pen he'd grown to associate with food, comfort, and security. But even if he may live longer in captivity, I'd never feel right about denying his wild instinct.

The possibility of Bugs suffering the consequences of freedom—death by predator—I tried to push aside.

Which brings me to my cats. Two of them were *not* rabbit killers—at least I'd never seen them with a rabbit in their jaws; they were big lazy housecats. The other two were convicted rabbit killers. Othello was getting old, though, and had lost his quickness. Boots, young and healthy, was the main concern, but I couldn't give him up; he was part of my animal family.

I'm aware my quandary could be seen as ridiculous by some. Doing right by my animals will always be my priority, though. And because they cannot tell me what they want, I have to rely on intuition.

I am utterly guilty of humanizing my domestic animals, but I knew I should not do so with Bugs.

❧ ❧ ❧

Spring brought another crop of wild baby rabbits, lying quietly in their unhidden and vulnerable nests. I waited with dread for the squeal of a captured baby rabbit. Sure enough, one afternoon at the end of March, Othello sauntered towards the house with a kit in his jaws, the air punctuated by those awful cries. Othello was no longer quick, but he was still observant, and a defenseless newborn rabbit was easy pickings.

I opened the front door to Othello waiting there patiently. It wasn't hard to release the kit from his jaws, and the squealing mercifully stopped. It was a precious ten-day-old bunny, but then I noticed with horror the back legs were paralyzed. Othello had damaged the baby's spine. I hardly had time to get angry at my killer cat before I heard another squealing baby, and looked up to see Sophie holding a kit in her jaws with what seemed to me a guilty air, as if she remembered this time last year how I'd yelled at her for her actions. The rabbit was likely from the same nest.

Again I had to think hard, to decide whether I could save two bunnies, one badly injured. I doubted the luck I'd had with Bugs would hold this time. All I'd read about why one should place kits back into their nest came back to me. I'd noticed Sophie wandering around the back of the house prior to her appearance in the front yard—this time I knew the vicinity of the nest. I secured the kit from Sophie's jaws, and now with two kits in my hands, carefully maneuvered the doorknob to get her and Othello inside, and started nest-hunting amongst the cedars behind our house. I stepped carefully, looking down for tiny bunnies remaining in a raided nest. It was nearing dusk, and I knew from my reading about cottontails that a mother rabbit returns to her nest at dusk. After looking fruitlessly for fifteen minutes, I found an out-of-the-way spot near a tree in the fence row, cleared some grass, and placed the two babies in their makeshift nest. Would the mother cottontail find babies that had been moved? Maybe not, but it was worth a try.

I didn't sleep well that night, wondering about the tiny lives. Adding to my concern, a misty rain started in the early morning hours, and I lamented the two getting wet and cold.

When I returned at dawn to the spot I'd placed them, there they huddled, just as I'd left them. Rain had started in earnest. The rain made my decision. I couldn't leave them in a downpour. In they came, to the master bathroom, and the hunt for a cardboard box began, followed by the mixing of kitten milk replacer, cream, and acidophilus.

They drank their replacer just as easily as Bugs had. Because they were older, with their eyes already open, they were a little warier than he'd been, but hunger overrode their fear, and they accepted my touch. I stayed quiet while feeding them, and kept hoping the kit who'd been injured would recover the use of its legs, but each day I'd grow more depressed seeing it pull itself along the floor of the box by its two front paws, its tiny back legs hanging limply. I couldn't hate Othello for doing what came naturally, but I sure was disappointed in him. The tiny brown eyes of the helpless kit seemed full of comprehension of her fate, trying to survive despite an injury that would prevent her from ever hopping again. I didn't check, but I thought of the tiny delicate kit as a female.

By the third day, although the injured kit had taken her formula daily, she started to fail. The injury affected her digestion, or her little spirit was destroyed. The evening of the third day, I found the sweetheart—she had the sweeter face of the two—lying on her back, breathing heavily, as if in distress. Her sibling, who had, until now, laid by her side, now lay several inches away, as if politely giving her room to suffer. I didn't know what to do. Even a vet would have no solution. I let her be. Again, I couldn't sleep.

The next morning at 8 a.m., when I lifted the towel that covered the box, I found the injured kit dead, lying on her side. Her sibling was resting quietly at the other end of the box, accepting death in the quiet way of rabbits.

The sweet-faced kit's earthly remains are near my garden, under a wisteria tree.

I watched the surviving kit grow under my care, a little less apprehensive than I was with Bugs, yet knowing death was a possibility. I checked and found she was a female, and picked the name Hazel from *Watership Down*. Hazel took to the syringe even better than Bugs had—or maybe it was my experience that made the feeding process easier. At any rate, as a team, we were adept. I'd learned since Bugs' babyhood that kits will accept tender leaves and grass as early as two weeks, so I left some wild lettuce and dandelion leaves in her box, and by the next day they'd disappeared. I gradually upped the amount of greens I fed daily, then in the next week introduced a few alfalfa pellets a day, following the formula/leaves/pellets routine until the middle of the fourth week, when she showed so much distress at being handled, I stopped feeding her formula.

I decided I would release Hazel. The only other option was building a new pen for her, and going through the same guilt wondering if I'd done the wrong thing holding her captive. I would find Hazel a safe place to be free. I wanted her to be fully prepared for release, though, so to transition her to the outdoors, I moved her to the hutch in Bugs' pen at the end of her fourth week. Mom was overjoyed at getting to use the shower in the master bathroom again, and I was amused at Bugs' excited response to smelling a female in his pen. Hazel's first evening in the hutch, I closed the door so Bugs couldn't get to her, although they could touch noses through the hail screen fence. She darted wildly, finding the perimeters of her hutch yard, before scrambling up the ramp to the hutch entrance and settling down in one of the nesting boxes, safe from Bugs' view. Bugs' mating senses, startled into action, fomented a compulsive hopping around the perimeter of the hutch. Cocoa didn't seem to care about Hazel.

I should mention there was another wrinkle: the week before I put Hazel in the hutch, I'd apprehensively removed the divider door in the pen so Bugs and Cocoa could share a bigger space to hop. I hoped that their time in a divided pen—eight months— may have created a positive change. Cocoa saw that Bugs was now bigger and even more feisty, less willing to be sexual prey. For a week, everything seemed good, and they each appeared content with their extra hopping space.

But it couldn't last. I discovered Bugs' shoulders bleeding one morning. Again! I felt like an idiot for assuming Cocoa would magically lose his horniness. Once again I found some hydrogen peroxide, and this time I had to perform first aid alone, but I got one direct pour on his shoulders before Bugs hopped away and hid out an entire day in the corner of the pen where I'd placed a shelter of cedar branches.

With this injury, a more permanent solution was in order: Bugs, the wild yet more well-adjusted, would get to stay in the bigger pen, and I'd build Cocoa a smaller "lean to" pen, as befitted his naughty self, by the side of the existing pen, using materials I had on hand. He'd still have more room than most domestic rabbits enjoy during their lifetime, I reasoned, and I'd make his pen comfortable, with all the same amenities he had in the bigger pen.

A couple of hours later, and voila—Cocoa would never harass Bugs again. This time I meant it. They *still* seemed to be drawn to each other, though: at dawn and dusk they hopped back and forth along the length of their common wall, touching noses through the hail screen.

Hazel liked to hide in her nesting box most of the time. I fed her pellets, greens, and tiny pieces of apple and banana. She graduated from a jar lid of water to a one-inch deep water dish during the four weeks she lived in the hutch.

The approach of hot weather spurred me to find a place to release her. Animal-loving neighbors Marilyn and Raymond, who lived only a couple of miles away, had seen my rabbit pen the year prior and now had a couple of rabbits of their own. They told me about a wild rabbit that came to the edge of their property and sometimes ventured near the rabbit hutches to eat the spilled alfalfa pellets. They didn't have cats, and their dogs were small and lived either indoors or contained in a fenced area. I asked if they'd let me release Hazel in their yard, and they agreed. On a pleasant spring afternoon, I took Hazel to their yard in a cat carrier, and released her near the tame rabbits' hutches. Hazel would enjoy the best of both worlds: freedom to find her own greens, and the cushion of backup rations in the form of stray alfalfa pellets under the hutches. The neighbors even placed a water bowl under a cedar tree for her, and on occasion I'd leave her a dish of fresh lettuce or a few blackberries.

The success of Hazel's release added fuel to my recognition that Bugs needed to run free.

And, another event swayed me: Cocoa appeared outside his pen one morning, hopping around nonchalantly. I couldn't believe my eyes. My two dogs pushed their way past me the second I opened the front door, in their usual rush to see what kind of sentry duty the morning would bring. Of course, they immediately saw Cocoa. Sophie rushed Cocoa the same way she rushed my cats, full-bore and seemingly hell bent, but stopping short of harm, revealing her innately gentle Lab nature. Cocoa took off like a flash, causing Opie, my little poodle, tail curled and ears perked, to give chase. I yelled "Stop!" but Opie was deaf to me. He knew he was in the wrong, though, and rolled over submissively when I caught up to him, letting me pick him up to put him inside. Sophie followed him in.

Then I investigated how Cocoa had escaped.

The hole wasn't hard to find—a large elm stood at one corner of the pen—one of the giant shade trees Bugs' pen and Cocoa's lean-to pen sat under. Cocoa had burrowed his way under a pallet within the pen, then out by the tree trunk. His derring-do impressed me, and he looked pleased with himself at having been the master of his own escape. However, I foresaw only trouble from my cats.

Catching Cocoa could provide an amusing sport for a younger person with more energy, but it made me feel like a fool. I knew rushing towards him would result in his running off, so I tried the quiet and patient approach, hoping to catch him unawares while his back was turned. I quickly saw this wasn't going to happen. Those eyes on either side of his head were useful, and seemingly he also possessed radar around his backside.

I had forgotten which of my cats were inside or outside that morning—easy to do when there's four of them—but I hadn't spotted any nearby, so I continued my patient circling around the yard to catch Cocoa, who studiously kept hopping a few feet out of my reach. Then my heart did a flip. The most ruthless of my hunters, Boots, materialized nearby on the picnic table, gazing intently at Cocoa's smooth brown form. I expected at any moment Boots would crouch into that distinctive pre-attack stance, sussing out his victim, then spring for the hapless Cocoa. Imagine my surprise when Boots flopped down, still gazing interestedly at Cocoa, but out of "attack mode," even when Cocoa hopped within a couple of feet of him! Then Othello, enemy of baby rabbits, appeared. Although I was sure he was unable at his age to catch a full-grown rabbit, I was just as wary. He immediately saw Cocoa, but as if picking up a cue from the nonchalant Boots, he stood stock still, observant, but obviously not in pursuit mode.

Cocoa, either realizing he was in the clear or too naïve to know better, continued hopping tauntingly back and forth within a yard of the duo.

I stood there flabbergasted. Could it be my cats, having seen Cocoa in his pen for so long, knew he was a pet and off limits? Or were they merely reigning in their instincts because I stood there? I'd just fed them their favorite mixed-grill canned Friskies, and their stomachs were full—maybe that was the key.

As an experiment, I started letting Cocoa out of his pen every few mornings for a supervised romp. Sometimes a couple of cats were outside, and though they'd approach Cocoa, they never lunged. Sophie the Lab would occasionally rush towards Cocoa in play, but wasn't serious about hurting him. Opie liked to chase, but would stop when I told him to. Cocoa's nonplussed demeanor around my cats, ignoring them while nibbling at grass, seemingly made him less enticing to them. Immediately upon being let out of his pen, Cocoa would head over to sniff the perimeter of Bugs' pen, rousing a heightened animation from Bugs that I took to mean he was jealous of Cocoa's freedom.

A scenario I'd read about at a discussion board about rabbit care—a glorious farmyard where tame rabbits hopped freely amongst cats—made me swoon with delight, and I wondered if I could pull off the impossible. Could both Cocoa *and* Bugs run free?

I saw after a couple of weeks that Cocoa's romps resulted in no calamities, and the idea of releasing Bugs took hold. I had to try it. I woke up one morning with a plan: All the dogs and cats would stay indoors, Cocoa would stay in his pen, and I would try what I'd been too scared to try for an entire year. I didn't tell my mother. She'd find out soon enough.

First, I fed Bugs and Cocoa their morning alfalfa pellets. Better for Bugs to leave on a full stomach, I reasoned.

I contemplated the possible outcomes of my plan: Bugs would be too scared to leave his pen. Or, Bugs would happily leave his pen, run off, and never be seen again. Or, Bugs would run off, hide in the huge mass of densely-thicketed and low-growing cedar bushes behind the house, amongst the trunks of elms, tall cedars, and catalpas in the small forest that bordered our property, where no cats nor dogs nor owls could harm him, and where he'd find cool shade in the summer and hollowed-out elm trunks for protection from the winter winds.

After foraging for himself for awhile, maybe he would come back to his pen. Or, barring a full return, Bugs would at least stay in sight. I'd keep dishes of pellets and water in a sturdy wooden box with a hole just big enough for him, under cover of the cedars. And, for extra protection, I'd build him brush piles. I knew just where I'd put them. Once in awhile at dawn or dusk, I'd see him grazing on clover and wild lettuce, and he'd let me approach to say "hi." I hoped for this scenario.

Every fiber of my being *willed* this scenario. I loved that rabbit. I couldn't bear the thought of losing him.

He finished his pellets and looked up. Out of habit, I almost went to pick him grass and clover. Bugs' inscrutable gaze focused on something I didn't see, and I lingered, knowing this could be the last time I'd see that face. His deep brown eyes seemed to reflect my apprehension. A gull's cry, unusual in our land-locked area, swung my attention towards the barn. The soaring eagle statue atop the weather vane pointed east. In Chinese Feng-Shui, east symbolizes the rabbit; in Celtic tradition, east symbolizes new beginnings.

Now or never.

I stood, approached the pen door from the inside, opened it and stepped out. Instead of closing and latching it as I'd done a thousand times before, I held it open. Wide open.

"Go on, little guy. You're free," I whispered.

Bugs approached the opening with trepidation, stretching his little body as I'd seen him do many a time.

The song of the universe must have reached a crescendo in those little ears.

Once he reached the threshold, he hesitated no more. Amidst the swallows' warbling and a soft wind breathing through the grass, he hopped out to his world.

Barn after roofing and painting

Eagle weather vane

Bugs on alert

One of several hideouts for Bugs behind house

Freedom

$\mathcal{E}$ P I L O G U E

After leaving his pen, Bugs lived where I'd hoped he would, in the forest-like growth of bushes and trees behind the house. He routinely visited a wooden box housing food and water, with a hole just big enough for him, that I'd placed under a dense undergrowth of cedar bushes near the house. Sometimes at dusk I'd spot Bugs nibbling a clover patch near those cedars; sometimes I spotted him further in the distance, near the corn crib, eating brome grass. Mom saw him one night in the driveway in her headlights, raised on his haunches, gazing at the rabbit pen where he'd once lived. How did we know it was him? Well, we'd never before seen a wild rabbit frequent the yard so consistently; plus, the button-size dark spot on his right flank helped identify him. If he was at a good distance and spotted me, he'd stop eating, stand stock-still, and let me watch him for a much longer time than a truly wild rabbit would. I knew my Bugs when I saw him.

Soon after Bugs' release, Boots spotted him too. I caught him starting a beeline in Bugs' direction. Putting my hand down directly in front of Boots' head, blocking him, and telling him "no" seemed to make him understand that rabbit was off-limits. But of course you can't take instinct out of a cat. To be safe, I made a habit of putting Boots inside the house before I took food and water to Bugs' shelter, made sure Boots was always well-fed, and kept his claws trimmed short. I compulsively created hideouts for Bugs in many places throughout the yard—brush piles and boxes that only he could fit into—and prayed that Bugs' vitality and wiliness would protect him.

Bugs' natural survival instincts kicked in. During the first few weeks, when I'd spot him behind the house and approach, he'd let me get within ten feet before hopping away. Several months later when I spotted him behind the house, he hopped toward cover the moment I called his name, his white tail flashing. "Excellent cottontail!" I chirped after him.

When winter approached, I spent a day making him an insulated shelter, roomy enough for a water and food dish with plenty of room left over for him to stretch out for a nap. I covered the shelter with metal roofing material, added a hinged tin roof, and filled it with dry brome hay for bedding. The final touch: Bugs' heating pad from the hutch; it ran from an extension cord off the east porch, and stayed in his box all winter.

During a full four months of fall and winter I didn't see him once, but I kept putting food and water out for him, and in late February I saw rabbit tracks in the snow leading to his shelter. Mice had discovered and invaded his shelter too; they ate his pellets, built a nest on top of his heating pad, and pooped in his food dish. But Bugs is a gentle soul, and probably didn't mind. He was out there in his backyard forest all along, biding his time until the clover would again grow fresh and sweet.

Then, the day before Easter 2014, near dusk, while I was transplanting some larkspur, Bugs appeared on the swell of ground behind our house where clover grew, munching away, looking at me briefly with his usual aplomb.

"Bugs! There you are!" I shouted in a gush of joy. He lingered for a full minute in the clover patch as if glad for the company, his fur exquisitely limned with rosy light of the setting sun, until Opie started barking in the distance and he hopped off into the trees.

I'm willing to bet Bugs didn't miss Cocoa, but maybe he'd meet up with that sibling of his I imagined, and they'd recognize each other and take turns standing sentinel while the other grazed.

The time might come when the stretches between spottings grows longer and finally stops, and I will always wonder what became of Bugs. For now, though, one thing's for sure: Bugs is keeping an eye out for mating partners. I hope he populates our yard with many progeny in the coming years. I'm ready to build brush piles to infinity.

For Further Reading

Adams, Richard. *Watership Down.*
London: Rex Collins Ltd., 1972.

Farmer, Steven. *Animal Spirit Guides.*
Carlsbad, CA: Hay House Publishing, 2006.

Lockley, R.M. *The Private Life of the Rabbit.*
New York: Macmillan, 1974.

Wild Mammals of North America: Biology, Management, and Conservation. Ed. by
George A. Feldhamer, Bruce C. Thompson, and
Joseph A. Chapman.
Baltimore: Johns Hopkins University Press, 1982.